SpringerBriefs in Education

Key Thinkers in Education

Series Editor

Paul Gibbs, Middlesex University, London, UK

This briefs series publishes compact (50 to 125 pages) refereed monographs under the editorial supervision of the Advisory Editor, Professor Paul Gibbs, Middlesex University, London, UK. Each volume in the series provides a concise introduction to the life and work of a key thinker in education and allows readers to get acquainted with their major contributions to educational theory and/or practice in a fast and easy way. Both solicited and unsolicited manuscripts are considered for publication in the SpringerBriefs on Key Thinkers in Education series. Book proposals for this series may be submitted to the Publishing Editor: Marianna Pascale E-mail: Marianna.Pascale@springer.com

More information about this series at http://www.springer.com/series/10197

Adam Dickerson

John Holt

The Philosophy of Unschooling

Adam Dickerson
Gundaroo, NSW, Australia

ISSN 2211-1921   ISSN 2211-193X (electronic)
SpringerBriefs in Education
ISSN 2211-937X   ISSN 2211-9388 (electronic)
SpringerBriefs on Key Thinkers in Education
ISBN 978-3-030-18725-5   ISBN 978-3-030-18726-2 (eBook)
https://doi.org/10.1007/978-3-030-18726-2

© The Author(s), under exclusive license to Springer Nature Switzerland AG 2019
This work is subject to copyright. All rights are solely and exclusively licensed by the Publisher, whether the whole or part of the material is concerned, specifically the rights of translation, reprinting, reuse of illustrations, recitation, broadcasting, reproduction on microfilms or in any other physical way, and transmission or information storage and retrieval, electronic adaptation, computer software, or by similar or dissimilar methodology now known or hereafter developed.
The use of general descriptive names, registered names, trademarks, service marks, etc. in this publication does not imply, even in the absence of a specific statement, that such names are exempt from the relevant protective laws and regulations and therefore free for general use.
The publisher, the authors and the editors are safe to assume that the advice and information in this book are believed to be true and accurate at the date of publication. Neither the publisher nor the authors or the editors give a warranty, expressed or implied, with respect to the material contained herein or for any errors or omissions that may have been made. The publisher remains neutral with regard to jurisdictional claims in published maps and institutional affiliations.

This Springer imprint is published by the registered company Springer Nature Switzerland AG
The registered company address is: Gewerbestrasse 11, 6330 Cham, Switzerland

Me schal worþe at your wille, and þat me wel lykez,

For I ȝelde me ȝederly ...

Sir Gawayn and þe Grene Knyȝt (III: 4)

Preface

> *It is the Age of Machinery, in every outward and inward sense of that word; the age which, with its whole undivided might, forwards, teaches and practises the great art of adapting means to ends. ... Thus we have machines for Education ... The time is sick and out of joint.*
> —Thomas Carlyle, Signs of the times, *The Edinburgh Review*, 1829

Sometimes, if it is looked at in the right way, the most trivial of remarks can reveal a whole ethos. It was the remark in the school newsletter that struck me this way. It was written as such communications typically are—brightly cheerful, with a faint undertone of menacing authoritarianism. It informed me that every day I should be reading to my children, *in order to improve their literacy skills* ("Be sure the experience is enjoyable, playful, and encourages children's active involvement; literacy should be engaging for your children, not a chore").

To borrow a phrase from George Orwell, that remark "reminds me, as Samuel Butler said of a cracked church bell he heard somewhere, of the smell of a bug" (Orwell 1970, p. 175). The person whose thought has helped me to articulate to myself just why this remark stinks, and precisely what the source of that stink is, is John Holt (1923–85). Holt was a critic of compulsory schooling and one of the 'fathers' of the modern homeschooling movement. But it was not those aspects of his work—significant though they are—that helped me to understand just what rang so discordantly in that remark in my children's school newsletter.

The problem, Holt suggests, lies in that little phrase 'in order to'; in the thought that in education, one engages in various activities *in order to produce learning*. To use the currently fashionable jargon, students in our 'learning institutions' engage in 'learning activities' in order to produce 'learning outcomes'. The learner's current activity is thus conceived of as an instrument for the production of some future state or capacity (knowledge, skill, etc.). The learner's activity is, that is to say, viewed as an efficient means to an end—its value lying not in the activity itself, but in the future outcome it is intended to bring about. Debates about education work overwhelmingly within this instrumentalist framework, concerning themselves with questions of the right means (e.g. pedagogical methods) and questions of the right ends (e.g. curricular content).

This essay is written in the conviction that Holt's work contains a philosophically rich and important critique of our culture's instrumentalist conception of the relation between activity and learning. This is not something that has been well understood about Holt's thought. But that, perhaps, is not surprising. After all, as philosopher Charles Travis remarks, "Sometimes an idea is so deeply engraved in the philosophic spirit of a time that it is difficult even to see it as a target, or as threatened, in cases where it is" (Travis 2000, p. xi). If anything is deeply engraved in the spirit of our time, it is instrumentalism: the thought that ends can be separated from means, and that human action must be considered as the pursuit of some desired future end that the action is calculated to produce. Indeed, as Marx pointed out long ago, at the heart of capitalism itself is the treatment of human activity as primarily instrumental. Except for the lucky few, we do not work because our work is worth doing for its own sake; we work because it is a necessary means to earning our living.

Holt's target is the idea that learning—at least if we wish to be 'effective' and 'efficient' in procuring it—is best thought of as something to be aimed at, intentionally and intelligently. Or, to express this target in the terms used above, it is the idea that the best route to learning is *education*—where by that term is meant the undertaking of certain activities *in order to* produce certain kinds of learning. In this book, I argue that Holt offers us a coherent philosophical critique of this apparently commonsensical thought. Stated summarily, the main points of his critique are as follows:

1. The best—most valuable, most significant—kind of learning is necessarily a *by-product* of activities (such as practices of inquiry) done for their own sake—we might say, out of a wholehearted *love* for the activities themselves.
2. That is, the best learning emerges (if all goes well) from *autotelic* activity, rather than from activity engaged in from instrumental motives (i.e. in which the activity is undertaken by the agent primarily as an efficient means to some desired external end).
3. Hence, the best learning cannot be aimed at intentionally; any attempt to do so is self-defeating.
4. The best learning involves not just growth in skills, knowledge and the like, but, overarching these, the development of certain character traits—the *virtues* of the activity in question. So, for example the virtues of inquiry include such character traits as curiosity, wonder, patience, imagination, determination and intellectual courage.
5. Conversely, to engage in activities in a way that is dominated by instrumental motives tends to be destructive of the agent's character. That is, such activity tends to be productive of the *vices* of the activity in question. In the case of inquiry, these vices include such character traits as passivity, incuriosity, rigidity, self-distrust and intellectual cowardice.
6. Furthermore, pursuing activities from instrumentalist motives tends to be destructive of the agent's pleasure (joy, satisfaction) in that activity.

If Holt is right, then the result of this argument is that education—at least, insofar as it is conceived of in instrumental terms—is not a good thing in the way we tend to think it is; that what it can achieve is limited in certain deep, conceptual ways; and that (to borrow a remark of Everett Reimer's) very important kinds of learning occur *in spite of* education, rather than *because* of it.

This essay could be termed an 'analytical reconstruction' of the argument sketched above, and thereby of Holt's philosophical views about the relationships between the concepts of *agency, activity, motivation* and *learning*. In taking this abstract focus, this essay necessarily leaves out of consideration many other valuable aspects of his work. Holt's books are full of empathic, richly detailed observations of children learning (or failing to learn); they also contain much wise discussion of the 'right relations' between adults and children, and practical advice for those involved in 'unschooling'. I hardly touch on this material. Nor do I deal with his bravely pioneering work on children's rights, or his broader discussions of the political economy of schooling.

So much for what I have not done. What I have done in this essay is to take Holt very seriously as a philosopher, who has things to say to us that we ought to listen to, whether we are ultimately persuaded by his arguments or not. We ought to listen to Holt precisely because his views go against the grain of our culture. They put into question the conceptual frameworks that tend to structure our thoughts about learning and education, and, in doing this, they help make visible the ruling prejudices of the time. That is, I think, just what philosophy ought to do—especially when, as seems so obviously the case to anyone with eyes to see, "the time is sick and out of joint".

Gundaroo, NSW, Australia   Adam Dickerson

References

Orwell, G. (1970). Letter to Brenda Salkeld, 7 March 1935. In S. Orwell & I. Angus (Eds.), *An age like this, 1920–1940. The collected essays, journalism and letters*, (pp. 174–5). London: Penguin.
Travis, C. (2000). *Unshadowed thought: Representation in thought and language*, Cambridge, MA: Harvard University Press.

Contents

1	**Only the Experts Shall Speak or Be Heard**	1
	1.1 Introduction	1
	1.2 Against Education	4
	1.3 Against Expertise	6
	1.4 Conclusion	13
	References	15
2	**The Spirit in Which the Work Is Done**	17
	2.1 Introduction	17
	2.2 Aristotelian Excursus, Part I: Activities	21
	2.3 Aristotelian Excursus, Part II: Virtues	23
	2.4 Aristotelian Excursus, Part III: Conclusion	29
	2.5 The Best Learning	32
	2.6 Unity and Fragmentation	37
	2.7 How Children Fail	40
	2.8 Drawing Together the Threads	42
	2.9 Stupidity and Intelligence	44
	2.10 Conclusion	49
	References	50
3	**Objections and Replies**	51
	3.1 Introduction	51
	3.2 Objection #1: Childish desires	51
	3.3 Objection #2: Disagreeable Hard Work	56
	3.4 Objection #3: Noble Savages	62
	3.5 Objection #4: Teachers and Teaching	70
	3.6 Objection #5: Utopianism	75
	References	76

4	**What Is to Be Done?**	79
	4.1 Introduction	79
	4.2 Shifting Strategies	81
	4.3 Homeschooling	85
	4.4 Conclusion	87
	References	91

Chapter 1
Only the Experts Shall Speak or Be Heard

> A life worth living and work worth doing—that is what I want for children (and all people), not just, or not even, something called 'a better education'. (Holt 1990a, p. 266)[1]

1.1 Introduction

John Holt (1923–85) was, during the 1960s and 1970s, the most famous radical critic of the US education system. His first book, *How Children Fail* (published in 1964) was a runaway best-seller. It has been continuously in print since first publication, it has sold well over a million copies, and has been translated into at least fourteen languages. In it, Holt argued that,

> To a very great degree, school is a place where children learn to be stupid. A dismal thought, but hard to escape. Infants are not stupid. Children of one, two, or even three throw the whole of themselves into everything they do. They embrace life, and devour it; it is why they learn so fast and are such good company. Listlessness, boredom, apathy—these all come later. Children come to school *curious*; within a few years most of that curiosity is dead, or at least silent. (Holt 1982, p. 263)

How Children Fail was the first of Holt's many books that criticised compulsory, coercive schooling. Indeed, Holt eventually came to reject the very idea of education itself, describing it as "learning cut off from active life" (Holt 1976, p. 3). Instead, Holt argued, "children want to learn about the world, are good at it, and can be trusted to do it with very little adult coercion or interference" (Holt 1981, p. 44). Hence, the idea of making children's lives revolve around 'educational institutions' is a bad one. As he wrote in the revised edition of *How Children Fail* (published in 1982),

> except in very rare circumstances the idea of special learning places where nothing but learning happens no longer seems to me to make any sense at all. The proper place and best

---

[1] In all quotations, emphasis is as in the original unless otherwise noted.

place for children to learn whatever they need or want to know is the place where until very recently almost all children learned it—the world itself, in the mainstream of adult life. (Holt 1982, p. 296)

For reasons I explore in this book, Holt argues that the best (most valuable, most significant) kind of learning takes place when that learning is, as it were, a *by-product* of 'active life'. Precisely what this comes to will be analysed in the chapters to follow, but it clearly means at least this: that such learning does not come about from activities undertaken primarily in order to produce certain learning outcomes. Rather, the 'best learning' comes from activities undertaken primarily because they strike the agent (the 'do-er' of the activities) as significant, valuable, or worthwhile in their own right.

Holt termed this approach to learning, *unschooling.* Since then it has also been called 'natural learning' and 'life learning'. However, as Holt himself implies in the passage just quoted, there is an important sense in which referring to this as a special 'approach to learning' is misleading. This is because learning in this way—learning as a by-product of taking part in the 'mainstream' of 'active life'—is as old as humanity. The purpose of giving it a name, and calling it *un*schooling, is to reclaim some of the territory of learning from the imperial tendencies of the 'schooling' paradigm. That is, there is a strong tendency for discussions about learning to be framed in terms of 'learning activities' undertaken in order to produce 'learning outcomes', the whole business being conducted in 'learning institutions' staffed by 'professional educators'—as if it were simply commonsensical and obvious that this is how learning *must* occur (at least, if it is to be achieved 'effectively' and 'efficiently').

Examples of this conceptual imperialism are easy to find; here I submit just one (taken more or less at random from the books before me). Consider this remark from the opening to Stewart Ranson's very influential work on 'lifelong learning', *Towards the Learning Society* (published in 1994). It begins with this large claim: "In periods of social transition, education becomes central to our future well-being". The justification for this claim is provided in the following sentence, which is as follows:

> Only if learning is placed at the centre of our experience can individuals continue to develop their capacities, institutions be enabled to respond openly and imaginatively to periods of change, and the difference between communities become a source of reflective understanding. (Ranson 1994, p. ix)

In other words, Ranson's argument is that because this is a period in which *learning* is particularly important, *education* must be 'central to our future well-being'. Here, in the move from one sentence to the next, we witness the act of 'education' (with its apparatus of institutions, policies, professional instructors, certification, and the rest) swallowing the entire semantic field of 'learning'. The thought that—as Holt suggests—some very important kinds of learning might best occur *outside* of the purview of educational professionals and educational institutions does not cross Ranson's mind.

1.1 Introduction

These views about how learning best takes place outside educational institutions, along with his tireless activism, made Holt a key figure in the history of the modern homeschooling movement. Towards the end of his book, *Instead of Education* (published in 1976), Holt wrote that,

> What most children need is a way of escape [from schools]. One of the things people could do who feel as I do about schools might be to help them find or make such ways. We once had a so-called Underground Railway (strictly illegal) to help slaves escape from slavery. Why not now a new Underground Railway, to help children escape from schools? ... [W]e have to blaze a new trail if only so that others may follow. The Children's Underground Railroad, like all movements of social protest and change, must begin small; it will grow larger as more children ride it. (Holt 1976, p. 218)[2]

After the publication of this book, Holt was contacted by early pioneers of homeschooling (which was, at this time, illegal in most US states). In response, Holt began to agitate on their behalf. Using the royalties from his works, he founded the magazine *Growing Without Schooling* (published from 1977 to 2001), which facilitated networking for homeschoolers, and contained legal advice, discussion and educational resources. In the first issue of this magazine, Holt wrote that,

> In starting this newsletter, we are putting into practice a nickel and dime theory about social change, which is that important and lasting social change always comes slowly, and only when people change their lives, not just their political beliefs or parties. (Holt 1999, p. 3)

In addition, Holt assisted with court cases and travelled around the US speaking on behalf of homeschoolers. In 1978, after some important legal victories by the homeschooling movement, *Time* ran a lengthy and sympathetic article on the topic, and Holt appeared on the popular 'Phil Donahue Show' to argue his case. This led to a tremendous increase in public awareness of homeschooling in the US, and marks its shift into the mainstream of ideas about educational alternatives (cf. Gaither 2008, pp. 122–8). The last book Holt published during his lifetime, *Teach Your Own* (1981), was a comprehensive discussion of homeschooling. Holt's influence on the homeschooling movement—particularly on its non-evangelical wing—remains significant (Stevens 2001). What is more, in marked contrast to many of the radicals of the 1960s and 70s, almost all of his books are still in print, decades after they were first published.

As even this very brief summary indicates, Holt's ideas about learning and education have had a substantial impact on the world; but despite this, those ideas have attracted very little *scholarly* attention. In the literature written and read by 'educational theorists' and 'philosophers of education' and suchlike, he is barely present. If one turns, for example, to standard contemporary surveys of educational thought, 'companions' to the philosophy of education, 'dictionaries' of educational thought and the like, it is rare to find Holt listed even once in the index—and careful, patient discussion and assessment of his ideas is almost entirely absent from the enormous

---

[2]N.B., Holt (1976) makes use of a distinction between 'S-chools' (compulsory, age-segregated) and 's-chools' (such as schools of music, dance, martial arts). As it is clear from the surrounding discussion which sort of school is meant, I have silently removed this distinction in all the quotes used from this work, as it would otherwise be distracting to the reader.

educational literature.[3] When Holt is mentioned at all, it is usually either with a passing sneer, or merely in reference to his historical influence on the homeschooling movement.

What are we to make of this silence, this absence? It is worth reminding ourselves that silencing, or rendering absent, is a standard part of scholarly practice. Scholars choose in their day-to-day work what to write about, cite, discuss, lecture on, include on student reading-lists. Through such acts they are simultaneously choosing what *not* to mention. In so doing, judgments are being made, implicitly or explicitly, about which views have the appropriate sort of value (as being 'respectable', 'scholarly', 'serious', 'legitimate', 'credible', etc.), and which do not. From the silence surrounding Holt's work, it is clear that his views have collectively been judged to be 'unacceptable'. That is, while it may be acceptable for a scholar to mention Holt as being of minor historical interest in terms of his influence on the homeschooling movement, it seems clear that his views are not seen as acceptable contributions to contemporary debates about learning and education. There are, I suggest, two reasons why this is so. The first reason is that, in criticising the very idea of education, Holt is attacking some of the most cherished beliefs of our age. However, more important than this is the second reason, which is that Holt's works are deliberately written in a form that rejects the implicit politics of the entire scholarly enterprise.

1.2 Against Education

One reason for Holt's neglect by scholars is surely a very simple and obvious one: that his central claim looks, on the face of it, to be preposterous. At the very least, it certainly flies in the face of deep-seated cultural beliefs. Holt, after all, argues that education—in the sense of undertaking activities, the primary purpose of which is to produce learning—is, in some important ways, a *bad* thing. But there is an almost universal consensus that education is a human good in an obvious and unqualified way, in need of neither justification nor argument. School attendance is, for example, taken as a measure of 'human development' by the UNDP, and thereby classed alongside other such obvious human goods as access to nutritious food, clean water, medical care, basic human security, and the like. Education is even enshrined as a human right, with Article 26 of the Universal Declaration stating that, "Everyone has the right to education". Governments around the world are obsessed with education—they spend a substantial part of the national budget on their educational systems, which is viewed as a necessary investment for achieving national prosperity in a highly-competitive, 'globalised' world. The "belief in education for growth" is, as Alison Wolf writes, "the great secular faith of our age. ... Questioning the

---

[3] The only monograph on Holt's work is Meighan (2007). Although this is a clear and helpful introduction, it does not move much beyond paraphrase.

1.2 Against Education

automatic value of any rise in the education budget, it seems, places one somewhere between an animal-hater and an imbecile" (Wolf 2002, pp. x–xi).

Education is also—or so it is widely held—a sort of social cure-all. It can create autonomous citizens and courageously critical thinkers out of the dependent, the childish, and the easily-led; it can empower women and girls to fight patriarchal oppression; education in tolerance will cure racism; education in civics will restore our faded democracies; education in sustainability will avert the ecological crisis, and so on and so forth. Thus secular saints such as Nelson Mandela can announce to almost universal acclaim that, "Education is the most powerful weapon which you can use to change the world". In the face of this, what sort of monster of reaction would dare criticise the idea of education?

Perhaps most importantly, education is apparently also the solution to poverty and inequality. In an updated version of the Victorian admonition to 'pull yourself up by your own bootstraps', the poor are told on all sides that what they need is *more education*—rather than, say, policies of genuine redistribution (as those benighted left-wingers of old had thought). It is certainly true that schooling has become a tremendously powerful social sorting mechanism (and class marker), with certified educational achievement, particularly from higher education, increasingly being a condition of access to decent work (a resource that grows evermore scarce). This social sorting is then justified by claims that more highly educated workers are more productive, and therefore are entitled to the higher incomes they tend to receive. The market, in other words, produces a *just* division of resources, with the most highly credentialed receiving the most. This is a meritocracy, we are told, in which (in the words of Thomas Frank), "You get what you deserve, and what you deserve is defined by how you did in school" (Frank 2016, p. 69).

There is thus a near universal consensus, transcending political differences, about the value and importance of education. In the face of this, it is unsurprising that Holt's critique has been met with silence from scholars (especially from those who work within university schools of education). Admittedly, the claims about an educational 'meritocracy' are, these days, starting to look a little—how should I put this?—*shopworn*. The escalating arms-race of educational credentialism is becoming harder to defend as an even remotely sensible use of social resources (cf. Labaree 1997, 2010; Caplan 2018). The 'deplorables', long stigmatised by the lack of the credentials possessed by their betters, are starting to make themselves heard, to the growing discomfiture of an increasingly discredited technocratic elite. But, nonetheless, the fundamental faith in education as an obvious human good remains largely undimmed.

However, this by itself is not enough to explain the scholarly silence around Holt's work. After all, many radical challenges to cultural orthodoxies receive a hearing in scholarship. Hence, I suggest that there is a further reason for why Holt's works are largely excluded from consideration. This lies in what I will call the *mode of telling* of Holt's works. This is worth discussing at more length, as it raises a number of important issues concerning the nature of Holt's project (and hence, the project of this book)—the nature of the claims that he makes, and the sorts of considerations that will count for and against them. That is, to use a bit of philosopher's jargon, it concerns the *epistemological* nature of what Holt is doing.

1.3 Against Expertise

Holt would have been neither surprised nor, I suspect, displeased by scholars' neglect of his work. He self-consciously wrote as an outsider to the establishment of 'educational experts' and had no interest in becoming an insider. Indeed, he cordially loathed the side of modernity that gives us the 'rational authority' of the certified expert, along with its associated practices of technocracy, managerialism, bureaucratisation, and 'meritocracy'. As he wrote in a response to Jerome Bruner in 1966:

> I know of no more mischievous idea, nor one more strongly deserving opposition, than this notion that, even on matters of common human experience, only the experts shall speak or be heard. (Holt 1966)

This is a strong and consistent theme in Holt's work. For example, twelve years later we find him writing in a letter to Ivan Illich that,

> the things which are more abstract and remote are valued much more highly, carry more credit with them, than things which people can learn from everyday life. I say this is a highly political decision and has highly political consequences. It diminishes the power, capacity, and self-respect of ordinary people. (Holt 1990b, p. 217)

The ways in which Holt's works are written reflect—or, better, *enact*—these deeply-held beliefs. After all, as Martha Nussbaum remarks, a mode of telling, "makes ... a statement about what is important and what is not, about what faculties of the reader are important for knowing and what are not" (Nussbaum 1990, p. 7). To put this another way, a mode of telling contains a *politics* of knowledge. Throughout Holt's works we thus find a mode of telling that is directly and deliberately opposed to the 'scholarly' or 'academic' mode.

The typical traits of the scholarly mode of telling can be swiftly itemised, as they are familiar to anyone who reads academic works. The scholarly mode tends to be dispassionate and impersonal in tone. It usually makes essential use of a specialised vocabulary, specific to the 'field' or 'discipline'. It tends to emphasise general, abstract statements over more particular, concrete ones. The implied author, or authorial persona, typically displays no signs of hesitation, puzzlement, or uncertainty, but lays matters out with a magisterial air. I use the term 'magisterial' quite deliberately. That we are dealing here with a politics of knowledge, and hence with questions of power, is clear from the tone. Where the scholarly tone is not that of the legislator or the judge, it is that of the prosecutor or the defending counsel: addressing the reader as a hostile sceptic, who needs to be convinced via argument—arguments conceived of as impersonal forces, rather than as an interaction between people. Power, of course, has institutional frameworks around it, and texts thus locate themselves in such frameworks through the manner of their publication (the scholarly

1.3 Against Expertise

journal, the university press, etc.), their look (down to the typography and cover design), and, perhaps most importantly, the way they place themselves within a web of other specialised texts via an apparatus of references and notes. In short, the scholarly mode claims a particular power, namely, the rational authority of the certified expert—an authority to which non-experts must defer on pain of irrationality—and addresses itself to other certified experts in its field.

The implicit picture of knowledge at work here is obvious enough. It is a mode of telling which suggests that experts in a given field possess a particular sort of knowledge that is scarce and valuable. This knowledge is scarce because it is significantly different from people's 'ordinary' or 'common-sense' understanding of things—that is, the sort of knowledge reached in familiar ways, through the exercise of familiar faculties, by 'ordinary people'. (For example, expert knowledge may require competence in certain kinds of complex theory, and/or involve the application of special methodologies in its production.) Because of its qualitative distinctness from 'ordinary' understanding, this expert knowledge is typically expressible only in a specialised, technical vocabulary, and comprehensible only to those who have successfully passed through a certain difficult process of scholarly training (a process which typically focuses on the ability to manipulate abstractions).

Hence, people can be publicly certified as being in possession of this scarce and valuable knowledge (e.g., by having a Ph.D. in the field), and this entitles them to be recognised as 'experts' who are then heard as speaking with particular *authority* about that aspect of the world. That is to say, the experts' words will tend to have a certain social power, while other voices (of those lacking the appropriate certification and recognition) will not possess that social power. So, for example, expert contributions in a given field are more likely to sway institutional decisions and policies, while the contributions of non-experts will tend to be silenced: ignored, ridiculed, treated as 'non-serious', and the like. In some cases, experts are even granted a legal monopoly of expertise over a certain field (enforced via professional associations, licensing laws, and the like). This deference to the experts in a given field is treated as purely rational—after all, if they have a monopoly of knowledge about the field, then it follows that only fools or charlatans would disagree with the experts. It also follows from this, that with regard to the field in question experts need only pay attention to contributions from fellow experts, and not to those made by 'ordinary people'. When speaking to non-experts, the 'appeal to authority' is the basic manoeuvre (i.e., 'you cannot understand the justification for this, so you have to take my credentials as a proxy for the strength of my argument and the quality of my evidence').

In contrast to this scholarly mode of telling, Holt's is a rhetoric that scrupulously avoids addressing us from a position of such expert authority. The implied author of his texts does not address us with a claim to possess a specialised knowledge, significantly different from our 'ordinary' or 'common-sense' understanding, and from a grasp of which we (the non-experts) are consequently excluded. The implied author is instead someone who invites us to stand beside him as a fellow inquirer; one whose manner suggests he is pointing out things that we can all see, if we only have the courage to be honest with ourselves, and exercise our ordinary capacities for attentive observation, reflective empathy, and thoughtful understanding.

This can be seen in a number of recurring features of Holt's works, of which perhaps the most salient is the way in which his characteristic form is not abstract theorising in a specialised jargon, but *narrative* told in a style almost exaggeratedly plain. Consider the opening paragraph of *How Children Fail*:

> I can't get Nell out of my mind. When she talked with me about fractions today, it was as if her mind rejected understanding. Isn't this unusual? Kids often resist understanding, make no effort to understand; but they don't often grasp an idea and then throw it away. Do they? But this seemed to be what Nell was doing. Several times she would make a real effort to follow my words, and did follow them, through a number of steps. Then, just as it seemed she was getting the idea, she would shake her head and say, "I don't get it." Can a child have a vested interest in failure? What on earth could it be? Martha, playing the number game, often acts the same way. She does not understand, does not want to understand, does not listen when you are explaining, and then says, "I'm all mixed up." (Holt 1982, p. 11)

Here we are a long way from a passage written in the typical scholarly mode. Holt's text is not discussing general, abstract truths about learning and failures to learn, but is telling us of a particular 'I' confronting two particular children ('Nell' and 'Martha') at a particular time ('today'). Note also the use of the interrogative form—these are, at this temporal point in the narrative, *real* questions, not rhetorical ones. We, the readers, are present with Holt and with his puzzlement, and the result is a text that often feels genuinely exploratory rather than declarative; a text in which time flows, rather than being written in the 'specious present' of the scholarly treatise; a text in which we accompany a mind engaged in the activity of inquiry, rather than listening to someone 'reporting back' *after* the inquiry has been completed.

This use of the narrative form, with its focus on the particular and concrete over the general and abstract, is characteristic of all of Holt's works, from his first book *How Children Fail* to his last, the posthumously published *Learning All the Time* (published in 1989). The opening line of that final book is, "Once I visited a family whose youngest child, then about five, I had not seen in several years" (Holt 1989, p. 2). Even in the case of Holt's most self-consciously theoretical and political work, *Freedom and Beyond*, we find that, again and again, the central concepts and distinctions are introduced by way of narrative episodes, and the discussion proceeds with narratives at key junctures. As the writer George Dennison observed, in his obituary for Holt, "He never derives theory from theory, but stays as close as possible to experience itself" (Dennison 1985, p. 8).

At this point it might be suggested that if Holt's writings are largely in narrative form, then this in itself constitutes a good reason for scholars to ignore them. After all—such an objection might run—this means that Holt's work consists, fundamentally, of nothing more than a collection of personal anecdotes (as argued, e.g., by Lister 1975, p. 11). Such anecdotes might make for entertaining reading, but they cannot possibly be a substitute for the sort of rigorous and systematic empirical evidence on which a theory of learning must be erected. As the popular phrase contemptuously puts it, "data is not the plural of anecdote". Hence, any broad ('theoretical') claims that Holt does make on the basis of such anecdotes, cannot aspire to anything beyond the level of cracker-barrel wisdom.

1.3 Against Expertise

A number of comments could be made about such an objection. To begin with, it is worth noting the elitism that makes the phrase 'cracker-barrel wisdom' a form of disparagement in their mouths. It is a sneer at the idea that ordinary people could possess any genuine knowledge of such matters. Holt, it should be said, explicitly referred to his own style as "cracker-barrel" (Armstrong 2013, p. 44)—wanting his work to be accessible to as broad an audience as possible.

More significant, however, is that this objection implicitly relies on a simple-minded positivism. It assumes that, in order to possess any 'theoretical interest', claims must rest on a foundation of systematic empirical evidence. But there are other sorts of tasks that we may want claims to do for us, and ones for which narratives may be well-suited. Narratives, with their focus on particulars, can be effective at changing how we see things; help us to see from new perspectives; help us reorder things we already know into new patterns that are fruitful in some way; and—perhaps most importantly—give us vivid 'reminders' of truths that, in a sense, we already know, but have failed to integrate into our understanding in the right sort of way. As Holt remarks in *What Do I Do Monday?*, "I am not trying to win an argument. I don't feel that I am *in* an argument. I am seeing something in a new way and I want to help others see it, or at least look at it, that way" (Holt 1970, p. 12).

If the narrative form of Holt's works, and his broader rejection of the typical scholarly mode, is not a good reason in itself for rejecting those works as 'serious' or 'acceptable' contributions to academic discussions of learning and education, it nonetheless helps to explain why Holt's voice is largely absent from those discussions. After all, the experts' claim to possess a certified rational authority to speak about a certain region of human life, is a claim to possess a *monopoly* of serious speech about those matters. And this is, of course, to claim that non-experts have nothing to say worth listening to about those matters. From this perspective, Holt's point-blank refusal to play the game of expertise-claiming (even to the extent of refusing to have the fact that he took a degree at Yale mentioned in his authorial biographical notes) means that he can be ignored, silenced, made absent from the discussion. The added facts that Holt sold so many books, and wrote in plain English for a general audience of 'ordinary people', provides further support for such a view.

Holt's own view on this is, of course, quite different. He suggests that learning is in fact something we all know a great deal about, and that therefore deferring to the credentialed 'experts' in this matter is a continuation of the stupefaction wrought by institutionalised schooling. As Holt remarks:

> Many people, speaking on a matter of common experience, in which their ideas are as likely to be as good as anyone else's, will begin by saying, "Of course I'm not an expert in these matters." Someone recently wrote that gerontology, the *nonmedical* study of old people, their lives, problems, and feelings, is a "new field about which nobody knows anything". What about all the old people? Don't they know something about it? Is their experience meaningless and worthless until some expert with a Ph.D. in gerontology explains it to them? Schools make knowledge scarce, make most of us think that what we know isn't true or doesn't count. (Holt 1976, p. 175)

In other words, to think that the non-scholarly mode of telling used by Holt is a good reason for ignoring his works, is precisely to beg one of the key questions at issue.

For it is to assume that *learning* is an area of human life in which the knowledge worth having must be a specialised, abstract knowledge. Of course, there are areas of human life where this assumption makes good sense. For example, if one considers, say, theoretical chemistry, or micro-particle physics, non-experts are highly unlikely to have anything useful to contribute. As Bernard Williams writes,

> The orderly management of scientific inquiry implies that the vast majority of suggestions which an uninformed person might mistake for a contribution to science will, quite properly, not be taken seriously and will not find their way to discussion or publication. Very rarely the cranky view turns out to be right, and then the scientists who ignored it are attacked for dogmatism and prejudice. But, they can rightly reply, there was no way of telling in advance that this particular cranky idea was to be taken seriously; the only alternative to their practice of prejudice would be to take seriously all such suggestions, and science would grind to a halt. (Williams 2002, p. 217)

From the perspective that views discussions of learning as the province of specialised 'scientific inquiry', Holt's views look like those of a crank (as Williams puts it), and can thus rightfully be ignored.

However, consider what becomes of this assumption if we instead hold the view, as Holt suggests we should, that learning is 'a matter of common experience'—like, say, *friendship* or *being a parent*. With regard to such matters, the notion of 'certifiable expertise' finds no purchase. After all, it would be a preposterous piece of scientistic hubris to claim that one could speak more authoritatively about such matters, on the basis of knowing some abstract 'theory' learned at a university. (As if there could be 'progress' in our knowledge about friendship or parenting, so that we moderns, if our practice is informed by the 'right theory', are now 'better' at being friends or parents than people in the past were!) It would be equally preposterous to think that any claims made about what friendship demands of one, or of how one should rightly relate to one's children, were admissible only if founded on 'systematic empirical evidence' (perhaps derived from a sociological survey meeting appropriate statistical measures of validity and reliability). Of course, this is not to say that if something is 'a matter of common experience' then all ideas about it will be equally good. Some reflections on the matter may be rich, wise, and profound; others stupid or superficial. But the test of the quality of those ideas will have nothing to do with whether they are conveyed in the typical scholarly mode, by an appropriately certified 'expert', rather than in Holt's own favoured narrative form.

So, is Holt correct in his claim that learning is a 'matter of common experience'? It seems doubtful that there exists a simple criterion by which such matters can be neatly demarcated from matters in which certifiable expertise makes sense. This book as a whole is an exploration of Holt's ideas, and will have to speak for itself as an argument for the value of his work. However, it is worth very briefly sketching two considerations in favour of his viewpoint.

First, one thing shared by those 'matters of common experience' mentioned above is that they are, in various respects, *ethically* inflected. That is to say, ideas of friendship and parenting deeply involve ideas about the *good* and the *bad*, the *right* and the *wrong*. As will be discussed in detail in the chapters to follow, Holt argues that the concept of *learning* is similarly ethically inflected in its content. It has, as we shall see,

1.3 Against Expertise

close connections to such concepts as 'the worthwhile', 'the valuable', 'the significant', 'the worthy-of-being-desired', as well as significant links with various virtues, and with love. Hence, Holt's works are, in an important sense, works in ethics—deeply concerned with issues of what he would term 'right relations' (between adult and child; between learner and the world; between the self and its own activity).

One of the noteworthy features of ethical concepts is that the notion of *expertise* makes no sense in relation to them (cf. Gaita 2004, pp. 100–9). It makes good sense to delegate questions about, say, how to design a power-plant, a bridge, or a jet engine, to those who are certified experts in such matters. But there are no 'ethical experts' to whom I can appropriately delegate my ethical decision-making, or who can legitimately claim a monopoly of serious (non-cranky) discussion of such matters. Of course this does not mean that there cannot be investigations of various kinds into ethical matters; but it does mean that such investigations will not look much like the 'scientific inquiry' discussed by Bernard Williams in the passage quoted above.

This leads me to the second reason for doubting the idea that discussion of learning should be restricted to appropriately certified experts. In order to legitimately claim a monopoly of 'serious' discussions about learning, such experts would need to possess a specialised knowledge or expertise about learning. This specialised knowledge would need to meet the following criteria:

(i) It could not be knowledge already possessed (implicitly or explicitly) by 'ordinary' people (for then the experts' claim to possess a monopoly of that knowledge would fall to the ground).
(ii) This knowledge would have to cover, if not all cases of human learning, at least a very wide variety of them. It would, in other words, have to take the form of a *general theory of learning*.
(iii) This knowledge would, at the same time as being very general, also have to be empirically applicable. So, for example, those possessing this knowledge would be able to design 'learning experiences' that were superior in delivering 'learning outcomes' compared to those designed by people who lacked this knowledge.

Knowledge meeting all these criteria would be a genuine 'learning science', with teaching being the 'applied science'.

Various educational theorists concerned to bolster the (always shaky) professional status of teaching have taken this picture very seriously indeed. John Darling, for example, writing of UK government attempts to wrest control of the school curriculum from the hands of the teaching profession, complains that, "Where a professional group has manifestly acquired a sophisticated critical understanding about X, it is hard to deny its right to exercise authoritative influence over how X is conducted" (Darling 1994, p. 110). But one must ask, have teachers and educational theorists *manifestly* acquired a *sophisticated critical understanding* of learning? Darling's anxiety that this acquisition is less than manifest betrays itself in the proliferation of meaningless value-claiming terms—and with good reason. As Holt himself would argue, being a good teacher is not a matter of possessing certified expertise in some 'science of learning'; it is not a matter of *skilled* performance or of the application of a *method* or *technique*. Rather, teaching is the "difficult art" (Holt 1976, p. 86) of relating to particular human beings in the right way. Along with a lively understanding of the subject matter being taught, it is therefore a matter of character traits, or virtues—such as patience, attentiveness, enthusiasm, charisma, and so forth (as David Carr has persuasively argued in a series of works; see, e.g., Carr 2004). It is, I take it, obvious that such virtues cannot be taught and certified in the way that knowledge of a 'general theory' can be.

The actual practice of teaching thus fails to support the idea that it is the application of some 'science of learning'. Furthermore, more general considerations suggest that the very idea of such a science is deeply problematic. This is because a general empirical theory of learning would have to operate at such a high level of abstraction that it would be emptied of any real empirical content. That is, it seems hard to imagine any kind of knowledge that could simultaneously meet both criterion (ii) and criterion (iii) above. Consider the extraordinarily wide range of 'objects' that can be learned. One can learn *that* various propositions are the case (e.g., that the freshwater lake with the largest area in the world is Lake Superior). One can also learn *how to do* a huge variety of things—how to tie one's shoelaces, how to operate a forklift, how to speak Tamil, how to cut tight dovetail joints, how to play jazz piano improvisation, how to do macroeconomic modelling, how to interpret philosophical texts, how to apply the Schrödinger equation in insightful ways in theoretical chemistry (and so on, and so forth). A general theory of learning would have to be abstract enough to deal with this extraordinary variety in the 'objects' of learning; however, if it was not to consist of empty truisms, the general theory would also have to be empirically applicable in some way. In particular, as noted above, it would have to lead to techniques and methods that improved learning.

The idea that there could be some general 'theory of learning' that could combine this level of abstract generality with actual empirical usefulness in educational practice, is extremely implausible. Unsurprisingly, as Christopher Winch argues, the main characteristic of the grand empirical theories of learning that have been proffered to date (e.g., behaviourism) is precisely their "uselessness" (Winch 1998, p. 183). Indeed, Winch suggests, "The possibility of giving a scientific or even a systematic account of human learning is … mistaken" (Winch 1998, p. 2). However,

> [This] should not be taken to imply complete pessimism about our understanding of learning. The cautions are more about the dangers of theory-building than they are about the possibility of understanding. What we need … are not more theories but more *description* and more *understanding* of what is already before us. In certain important respects, the theories stand in the way of our understanding. (Winch 1998, pp. 2–3)

The theories stand in the way of our understanding. I think Holt would have been deeply sympathetic to this remark, with its echo of Wittgenstein. Holt fought hard for his first book to be entitled '*How* children fail' against his publisher's preference that it be called '*Why* children fail' (Holt 1990c, p. 123). Asking 'Why?' in this context is the wrong question. It is to ignore the details of what lies before us—as if we already knew what it is for children to succeed or fail at learning—and jump straight to causal theorising. Asking 'How?', on the other hand, is to focus first on the careful observation and scrupulous description of the phenomena—precisely what Winch suggests we need when it comes to understanding the nature of learning. As Holt writes in his second book, *How Children Learn*, "My aim in writing [this book] is not primarily to persuade educators and psychologists to swap new doctrines for old, but to persuade them to *look* at children, patiently, repeatedly, respectfully …" (Holt 1983, p. 271).

A number of the issues I have touched on above will be returned to, and elaborated upon, in the chapters to follow, but let us, for the time being, draw this discussion to a close. I have suggested that a key reason for the scholarly silence around Holt's works—despite their very real impact on the world—is their mode of telling. That is, his works are written in deliberate opposition to the scholarly mode and its epistemological, ethical, and political presuppositions. At this point two obvious objections raise their heads. The first is that this book, in which I analyse Holt's ideas, *is* written in the scholarly mode—so is that not inconsistent, or at least in tension, with what I have just said about the nature of Holt's works? There is a certain truth to this objection; and I would be the first to concede that in a 'translation' like this there is a loss. However, I hope that there will also be gains—in helping to make Holt's works visible to people to whom, at present, they are invisible. In the words of Stanley Cavell, "Criticism is always an affront, and its only justification lies in its usefulness, in making its object available to just response" (Cavell 1976, p. 46). Readers can judge for themselves whether they think this book was useful in that way.

This leads me to the second objection, which is that, in 'translating' Holt in this way, am I not making him out to be a purveyor of precisely one of those 'general theories of learning' that I criticised above? This objection is misguided. The analytical account that is given in the following chapters is a work in *philosophy*—not, for example, in empirical psychology. Philosophy, as I understand it, is not a technical, 'scientific' discipline that leads to 'results' and 'findings'; it is (in the words of Talbot Brewer) "a focussed effort to examine one's own concerns, bring them to articulacy, and see whether they can stand up to reflective scrutiny" (Brewer 2009, p. 10). For this reason, philosophy is the possession of all people willing to engage in it, not the specialised province of credentialed experts in universities. Hence, the discussion of Holt's ideas developed in the chapters to come has no grand empirical theory of learning to offer, and does not rely on causal claims supposedly established through specialised experimental methods. Rather, it appeals only to reasoning and to conceptual resources that lie ready to hand. In this way it is, I hope, open to all comers.

1.4 Conclusion

As remarked, I have written this book to recuperate, clarify, and explore Holt's views about the nature of learning and education. In order to do this, the book undertakes what could be termed an 'analytical reconstruction' of the argument that lies at the ground-floor of Holt's thinking. As discussed above, like Holt the discussion will treat learning as a 'matter of common understanding', in that what is needed in order to understand its nature is not causal theorising, but rather an approach that examines and assesses the conceptual resources already present (even if only inarticulately) in our own understanding. That is to say, what is needed is a philosophical analysis of Holt's account of learning, and of the accompanying family of concepts such as *desire*, *motivation*, *activity*, *virtue*, and *pleasure*. That analysis is what this book attempts to provide.

In approaching matters this way, the book thus treats Holt's views of learning and education as essentially static, rather than dynamic. This is not just a simplification made for the sake of making exposition easier. Holt had a long career of writing and activism, and of course a number of his views shifted in significant ways over that period. However, all of his writing is ultimately animated by one and the same underlying account of learning. Holt certainly expressed this view with greater clarity and articulacy over time, but, nonetheless, it remains, in its fundamentals, the same from *How Children Fail* until his final work. Hence, my explication does not follow the *historical* development of Holt's thought, but draws on his works in whatever order best suits the needs of my analysis.

By viewing his core ideas as static in this way, this book does not attempt to relate Holt's views to their changing historical context, and the tactical demands of the various debates and polemics into which they were inserted. Such an approach would require, at the very least, placing his writings in relation to the rise and fall of the 'counter-culture' and the New Left in the USA over the 1960s and 1970s. This in turn would mean reading Holt in the company of important works by other radical critics of education of the period, such as Goodman (1971), Illich (1971, 1981), Dennison (1969), Herndon (1965, 1971), Reimer (1971), Postman and Weingartner (1971), and Kohl (1971). It would also involve examining systematically how his ideas relate to earlier bodies of thought such as that of Deweyan progressivism, anarchism, and the American tradition of 'self-reliance'. A little of this work has been done (see the discussions of Holt in Miller 2002, Chap. 3; Olson 2011, pp. 27–32; Bickman 2003, pp. 142–5) but it is not the approach that this book will take. My aim here is to provide a clear articulation of Holt's underlying thought, rather than a detailed tracing of lines of historical influence.

Viewed analytically, Holt's body of work can be seen as composed of three components, as follows.

[1] There is a *positive* or *constructive* account of what the best (most valuable, most significant) sort of learning is, and the conditions conducive to such learning.
[2] Based on this positive account, there is a *critique* of instrumentalist practice in education, arguing that the structural features of that practice are such that it is, intrinsically, in tension with, or hostile to, the sort of 'best learning' analysed in [1].
[3] Various *practical strategies* are discussed for mitigating the problems with education analysed in [2], and for achieving the sort of 'best learning' analysed in [1].

1.4 Conclusion

In many of Holt's works, the practical strategies (the third component) is where the main focus lies. This is unsurprising, given that he wrote not for the sake of theorising, but primarily as a form of activism—to change people's lives. This is also where the key shifts in his thought occurred over time, as he moved from advocating school reform and learner-centred pedagogy, to a radical rejection of compulsory education and advocacy of homeschooling. However, the main focus of this book will be on articulating, analysing, and clarifying Holt's positive account of learning (the first component), and his critique of education (the second component). These will be treated together, as much of Holt's positive account is expressed by way of his critique (that is, it is often in the reasons he uses to justify his critique that we find his positive account).

The plan of the rest of this book is as follows. In the following chapter (Chap. 2) I give an outline of Holt's positive account of learning, and how it functions to support his critique of education. Next (Chap. 3), I fill in this picture by way of considering some objections that are likely to be raised against it. Finally, (Chap. 4) I briefly consider Holt's suggested practical strategies in the light of the analysis developed in the previous chapters.

References

Armstrong, T. (2013). Cracker barrel writing. In P. Farenga & C. Ricci (Eds.), *The legacy of John Holt* (pp. 41–6). Medford, MA: Holt GWS.
Bickman, M. (2003). *Minding American education: Reclaiming the tradition of active learning*. New York: Teachers College Press.
Brewer, T. (2009). *The retrieval of ethics*. Oxford: Oxford University Press.
Caplan, B. (2018). *The case against education: Why the education system is a waste of time and money*. Princeton, NJ: Princeton University Press.
Carr, D. (2004). Rival conceptions of practice in education and teaching. In J. Dunne & P. Hogan (Eds.), *Education and practice: Upholding the integrity of teaching and learning* (pp. 102–15). Oxford: Blackwell.
Cavell, S. (1976). *Must we mean what we say?* Cambridge: Cambridge University Press.
Darling, J. (1994). *Child-centred education and its critics*. London: Paul Chapman.
Dennison, G. (1969). *The lives of children: The story of the First Street School*. New York: Random House.
Dennison, G. (1985). Statement. *Growing Without Schooling, 48*, 8. Available at https://issuu.com/patfarenga/docs/gws-48. Accessed April 2019.
Frank, T. (2016). *Listen, liberal: Or, whatever happened to the party of the people?* New York: Metropolitan Books.
Gaita, R. (2004). *Good and evil: An absolute conception* (2nd ed.). London: Routledge.
Gaither, M. (2008). *Homeschool: An American history*. London: Palgrave Macmillan.
Goodman, P. (1971). *Compulsory miseducation*. Harmondsworth: Penguin.
Herndon, J. (1965). *The way it spozed to be*. New York: Simon and Schuster.
Herndon, J. (1971). *How to survive in your native land*. New York: Simon and Schuster.
Holt, J. (1964). *How children fail*. New York: Pitman.
Holt, J. (1966). On education: An exchange between Jerome Bruner and John Holt. *The New York Review of Books*, 12 May.
Holt, J. (1970). *What do I do Monday?* New York: E. P. Dutton and Co.

Holt, J. (1976). *Instead of education*. New York: E. P. Dutton and Co.
Holt, J. (1981). *Teach your own: A hopeful path for education*. Liss, Hants: Lighthouse Books.
Holt, J. (1982). *How children fail* (revised ed.). New York: Merloyd Lawrence.
Holt, J. (1983). *How children learn* (revised ed.). London: Penguin.
Holt, J. (1989). *Learning all the time*. New York: Merloyd Lawrence.
Holt, J. (1990a). Letter to Susannah Sheffer, 12/29/83. In S. Sheffer (Ed.), *A life worth living: Selected letters of John Holt* (pp. 263–7). Columbis, OH: Ohio State University Press.
Holt, J. (1990b). Letter to Ivan Illich, 5/24/78. In S. Sheffer (Ed.), *A life worth living: Selected letters of John Holt* (pp. 213–20). Columbis, OH: Ohio State University Press.
Holt, J. (1990c). Letter to Betty Rivard, 10/20/72. In S. Sheffer (Ed.), *A life worth living: Selected letters of John Holt* (pp. 123–5). Columbis, OH: Ohio State University Press.
Holt, J. (1999). On social change, August 1977. In Holt Associates (Eds.), *Growing without schooling: A record of a grassroots movement. Volume 1, August 1977–December 1979, GWS#1–12* (pp. 3–4). Cambridge, MA: Holt Associates Inc.
Illich, I. (1971). *Deschooling society*. Harmondsworth: Penguin.
Illich, I. (1981). *Shadow work*. London: Marion Boyars.
Kohl, H. (1971). *36 Children*. Harmondsworth: Penguin.
Labaree, D. F. (1997). *How to succeed in school (without really learning): The credentials race in American education*. New Haven: Yale University Press.
Labaree, D. F. (2010). *Someone has to fail: The zero-sum game of public schooling*. Cambridge, MA: Harvard University Press.
Lister, I. (1975). The challenge of deschooling. In I. Lister (Ed.), *Deschooling* (pp. 1–15). Cambridge: Cambridge University Press.
Meighan, R. (2007). *John Holt*. London: Continuum.
Miller, R. (2002). *Free schools, free people: Education and democracy after the 1960s*. New York: State University of New York Press.
Nussbaum, M. C. (1990). *Love's knowledge: Essays on philosophy and literature*. Oxford: Oxford University Press.
Olson, K. (2011). *Schools as colonizers: The deschoolers of the 1960s*. Saarbrucken: VDM Verlag Dr Muller.
Postman, N., & Weingartner, C. (1971). *Teaching as a subversive activity*. Harmondsworth: Penguin.
Ranson, S. (1994). *Towards the learning society*. London: Cassell Education.
Reimer, E. (1971). *School is dead*. Harmondsworth: Penguin.
Stevens, M. (2001). *Kingdom of children: Culture and controversy in the homeschooling movement*. Princeton, NJ: Princeton University Press.
Williams, B. (2002). *Truth and truthfulness: An essay in genealogy*. Princeton, NJ: Princeton University Press.
Winch, C. (1998). *The philosophy of human learning*. London: Routledge.
Wolf, A. (2002). *Does education matter? Myths about education and economic growth*. London: Penguin.

Chapter 2
The Spirit in Which the Work Is Done

> It is love, not tricks and techniques of thought, that lies at the heart of all true learning. (Holt 1983, p. 303)

2.1 Introduction

This chapter is the heart of the book. It analyses the conceptual structure that underpins Holt's account of learning and his critique of education. One way to view this analysis is as the solution to an interpretative problem. After all, the exceptional clarity and plainness of Holt's prose can hide the fact that his central claims about learning and education are, *prima facie*, rather puzzling. To bring out this interpretative problem, I begin by considering the contrast Holt draws in the following passage. This is quoted from the opening chapter of *Instead of Education*; Holt sees fit to repeat it *verbatim* five years later in *Teach Your Own*, so it can be considered as being, as it were, a canonical text.

> This is a book in favor of *doing*—self-directed, purposeful, meaningful life and work— and *against* 'education'—learning cut off from active life and done under pressure of bribe or threat, greed and fear. (Holt 1976, p. 3)

Replacing the polemical terms 'bribe' and 'threat' with more colourless language, Holt is thus defining *education* as activities, deliberately designed to produce learning, which the agent is primarily motivated to undertake by incentives and/or disincentives that are external to the activity. That is, the activity is not undertaken by the agent because it strikes her as valuable, significant, or worth doing in its own right, but because it is a means of avoiding some disincentive ('threat') and/or achieving some incentive ('bribe'). In contrast, what Holt calls *doing* consists of activities that the agent undertakes precisely because they do strike the agent as worth doing in their own right; in this way, such activities are genuinely self-directed.

It is worth emphasising how Holt's definition of 'education' focuses on the motivational or evaluative outlook of the *learner* (the 'agent' referred to above). Contrast this focus, for example, with that implied in R. S. Peter's well-known remark that the concept of education "implies that something worth while is being or has been intentionally transmitted in a morally acceptable manner" (Peters 1966, p. 25). The notion of *intentional transmission* takes for granted what could be termed a 'top-down' perspective on education. It is the perspective of the teacher, the curriculum designer, the educational policy maker; for it is they who intend to transmit learning via educational activities. Holt's definition, on the other hand, focuses our attention on how the activities appear from the perspective of the agent—the child, the learner, the student—who is undertaking those activities.

This thus begins to explain the importance of the concept of the learner's *freedom* for Holt's account. Freedom is, as it were, a test for discovering the kind of motivation that is moving the agent to undertake the activity. It is a way of posing this question: would the agent continue to undertake a particular activity if she were free—that is to say, *in the absence of* external incentives and disincentives ('bribes' and 'threats')? If so, then the activity in itself is sufficient to motivate the agent; that is, the activity strikes the agent as valuable or significant enough to be worth doing in its own right.

We can say, then, that *education* is effectively defined by Holt as the undertaking of 'learning activities' that would *not* be undertaken by the agent if she were free from the influence of external incentives and disincentives. What are we to make of this, *qua* definition? It is clear that it is not intended 'analytically'—that is, to provide necessary and sufficient conditions for capturing all uses of the English word 'education'. After all, this word can be used in a very broad way, where it is virtually synonymous with 'learning'. It can also be used much more narrowly, to refer to particular activities that occur in institutions officially designated as 'educational', under the guidance of those officially recognised as professional educators (as in 'I received my education at Eton and Oxford').

In giving his polemical definition of education, Holt is not, of course, attempting to capture the 'logical essence' of the concept in some 'value-free' way; rather, he is using it to draw our attention to a pervasive empirical feature of the actual practice of many of our educational institutions. This pervasive—and, I would suggest, obvious—feature is simply this: typically, the 'learning activities' that go on under the auspices of these institutions are *not* such that the agent (child, learner, student) would be motivated to undertake those activities, in the absence of external incentives and/or disincentives. That is, typically, the activities *in themselves* would not strike the agent as sufficiently valuable or significant enough to be worth doing.

Those who find this claim about our educational institutions to be an unfair caricature, should consider the following. Think of all the 'learning activities' that go on, year after year, at all levels of the education system—the books read, the class discussions had, the essays and papers written, the worksheets filled out, the exams taken. Then ask yourself, how much of this activity would be undertaken by students in the absence of external incentives and disincentives ('bribe' and 'threat', as Holt puts it)? That is, if there were no marks, gold stars, places on the Honour role, high school certificates or university degrees to be gained by undertaking the activity; if there was no potential of the humiliation of a failing grade, a teacher's anger, a parent's disappointment, if one did not undertake the activity. The answer, I suggest,

2.1 Introduction

is obvious. In the absence of external incentives and disincentives, very, very little of that activity would be undertaken: the exams would not be sat; the essays would largely remain unwritten; almost all the worksheets would be left blank.

We now need to examine just what Holt thinks is wrong with this situation. After all, an easy retort to having this pervasive feature of our educational institutions pointed out would simply be: *So what? For*, it might be said, *people—and children in particular—often need external incentives and disincentives to encourage them to do what is in their long-term interest.* Holt's account of what is wrong with education (by which is meant, that pervasive feature of actual educational practice) is where matters become both more interesting and more puzzling.

For a start, it is important to emphasise that his objection to education is not simply the fact that it denies the learner self-direction (freedom, autonomy). That is, Holt is not giving a *libertarian* critique of education. This can be seen, for example, in the following important summary statement:

> The main reason for giving young people self-direction, autonomy, and choice in their learning is … quite simply because that is how people learn best. Everyone. All the time. (Holt 1972, p. 4)

Note the structure of Holt's reasoning in this passage. Holt's argument does not terminate with an appeal to the supposedly self-evident value of 'self-direction, autonomy, and choice', as it would if he were arguing on libertarian grounds. Rather, he states that such freedom is important *because* it is a condition that people require in order to 'learn best'.

Holt's critique is thus the paradoxical-sounding claim that *education is bad for learning*. To spell this out a little more precisely, his claim is as follows. The use of external incentives and disincentives to motivate agents to undertake 'learning activities' is a bad thing. It is a bad thing because acting from this sort of motivation is hostile to, or in tension with, acquiring the best (most significant; most valuable) kind of learning. (Just what that learning is, and what is 'best' about it, is of course one of the central topics of this chapter; but, for the time being, I will leave its nature unspecified.) Indeed, Holt goes further than this. Not only is education hostile to the acquisition of the best sort of learning, it in fact tends to be damaging to the agent *qua* inquirer. As Holt famously writes in *How Children Fail*, "To a very large degree, school is a place where children learn to be stupid" (Holt 1982, p. 263). (And just why Holt argues this will be another of this chapter's topics.)

To return to the initial contrast with which this discussion began, the way to acquire the best sort of learning is, Holt argues, not *education* but *doing*. That is, the best learning is acquired through what, as we have seen, he variously describes as "self-directed, purposeful, meaningful life and work", "active life", and "work worth doing". These are activities which are undertaken because they strike the agent as significant, valuable, or worthwhile in themselves (or, in their own right). Here, the phrase 'in themselves' means partly that those activities are undertaken independently of external incentives or disincentives—that is, they would be undertaken even if the agent were 'free'. However, it also means that these activities are not undertaken in order to produce learning—that is, they are *not* undertaken *as* 'learning activities'.

For to undertake an activity as a learning activity, is to undertake it as an efficient means to an end—the end being the learning that it is intended to produce. In turn, that means that the agent is not undertaking the activity because it strikes her as being worth doing in itself; rather, she is doing it merely as a 'model' or 'exercise' for the purposes of learning. Hence, Holt is claiming that the best sort of learning can be acquired only by undertaking activities that do not aim at learning. Rather, as he puts it, the most valuable sort of learning is acquired by the agent "naturally, incidentally, as a *byproduct* of doing or attending to something important to him" (Holt 1971, p. 72; my emphasis).

I am now in a position to lay out the interpretative problem that the rest of this chapter will set about trying to resolve. Ideally, we would like an interpretation of Holt's views that will allow us to make good sense of the following claims:

1. There is a kind of learning that is particularly valuable, important, best, or 'true'.
2. This 'best learning' is a *by-product* of activities that an agent undertakes because *the activity in itself* strikes the agent as worth doing.
3. This 'best learning' is, in fact, *essentially* (i.e., necessarily) a by-product of such activities.[1] This is because for an agent to undertake an activity with the aim of producing learning (i.e., to undertake it as a 'learning activity') is *ipso facto* not to undertake the activity because the activity *in itself* strikes the agent as worth doing.
4. Therefore, the attempt to produce this 'best learning' through activities that are motivated via external incentives and disincentives—including the incentive that the activity is an efficient means to produce learning—is intrinsically self-defeating.
5. Therefore, education is intrinsically hostile to the acquisition of this 'best learning'.
6. Furthermore, education also has an intrinsic tendency to be damaging to the agent *qua* inquirer.

This puzzling argument all hangs on the *motivational structure*, or *evaluative outlook*, of the agent. Holt's argument, after all, is claiming that the sort of learning—and the *value* of the learning—that one can gain from an activity, is deeply linked to the agent's motivations for undertaking that activity; or, equivalently, with how the agent evaluates that activity. That is, the crucial question for Holt is *how* the activity shows up for the agent as worth doing. For example, is the activity worth doing only in order to receive a 'bribe' or avoid a 'threat'? Or would the agent choose to do the activity independently of any such external incentives and disincentives?

The rest of this chapter is an attempt to make good sense of this argument, by examining the philosophical substructure that underpins and connects its premises and conclusions. To keep the exposition as clear and uncluttered as I can, I begin by working at quite a distance from Holt's texts, in order to build an analysis of the key

---

[1] The general idea of 'states that are essentially by-products' of activity, I take from the superb analysis in Elster (1983), Chap. 2.

2.1 Introduction

conceptual links between *activity*, *agency*, and *learning*. In the later sections of the chapter, I then return to the texts with this analytical model in hand, to show how it can illuminate his claims.

2.2 Aristotelian Excursus, Part I: Activities

In building this analytical reconstruction of the underpinnings of Holt's views, I will be making use of conceptual resources drawn from other philosophers. In particular, I will be making use of concepts drawn from Aristotle's *Nichomachean Ethics*, and the works of two modern Aristotelians, Alasdair MacIntyre and Talbot Brewer. It should be noted that I appeal to Aristotelian resources simply because they will help to clarify the issues at stake; their use is not intended as a claim that they had any direct influence on Holt's works. Indeed, I can find no evidence in Holt's corpus that he ever read a word of Aristotle. However, consider Holt's repeated emphasis on a life composed of 'doing', of the human need for "serious, difficult, demanding work" (Holt 1990, p. 251), and his remark that,

> By 'work' I meant and still mean … what people used to call a 'vocation' or 'calling'—something which seemed so worth doing for its own sake that they would gladly choose to do it even if they didn't need money and the work didn't pay. … [T]o find our work, in this sense, is one of the most important and difficult tasks that we have in life. (Holt 1981, pp. 169–70)

These are deeply Aristotelian thoughts. For both Aristotle and Holt, the human good does not involve acquiring a bundle of capacities (skills, knowledge), but from *actualising* those potentialities in activities—in particular, in activities that are worth doing in themselves. Hence, as Holt puts, any 'life worth living' will, crucially, involve 'work worth doing', where this means (as the passage quoted above emphasises), worth doing for its own sake, and not simply because it is a means of acquiring such external goods as money, power, or status. In more Aristotelian terms, the good (*eudaimon*) life is made up of *autotelic* activity, rather than *instrumental* activity. In thinking through the implications of this view of the human good for learning and education, Holt is responding to the deep connections between concepts like motivation, agency, and activity. In the *Nichomachean Ethics*, Aristotle gives us a rich account of precisely those connections, and that work thus provides important resources for making sense of Holt's views.

I will begin by focussing on the nature of *activities*; a term that has so far been left unanalysed. A rough-and-ready distinction can be drawn between two kinds of human activity. On the one hand there are activities in which there are *not* multiple dimensions of *excellence* in that activity. These are, for example, simple activities that are fully rule-governed or 'algorithmic' by nature, and which are therefore either done correctly or incorrectly. Consider such activities as counting whole numbers; making simple arithmetical calculations; giving memorised answers to standardised questions; spelling words correctly. Or, to take another sort of example, they are mundane activities which we have no interest in making fine judgments of excellence about—they are either done acceptably, competently, or not. Consider such activities as tying one's shoelaces, brushing one's teeth, or washing the dishes. In many cases, such activities can be done, by an experienced agent, 'mechanically', 'on auto-pilot', or 'without thinking about them'. That is, once they are learned, the competent doing of such activities typically calls for no particular quality of attention from the agent.

On the other hand, there are human activities which (roughly following MacIntyre's usage) I will call *practices* (see MacIntyre 1984, pp. 187–8). The key distinguishing feature of practices is that they have internal standards of excellence in many dimensions. To engage with excellence in a practice (that is, to produce excellent examples of that practice) cannot be achieved by the blind, mechanical, or unthinking application of rules; rather, it requires the exercise of judgment in a way that is indefinitely sensitive to context. Furthermore, the standards of excellence specific to a given practice are discovered through doing the practice, and cannot be stated independently of the practice. As MacIntyre puts it, this is to say that practices have *internal goods*. What is more, assuming all goes well, one's grasp of the internal goods of a practice develops as one becomes more adept and experienced at that practice. What begins as a relatively inchoate, crude, or inarticulate intimation of the standards of excellence of a practice slowly becomes, *through engaging in that practice*, clearer, and more ramified, articulate, subtle, nuanced and complex. As MacIntyre puts it, by engaging in a practice "human powers to achieve excellence, and human conceptions of the ends and goods involved, are systematically extended" (MacIntyre 1984, p. 187). To use Brewer's term, this is to say that practices are *dialectical*. As he writes, in a practice there is a

> dialectical interaction between one's intimations of how best to carry forward with the activity, and a series of reifications of these intimations in the form of stretches of activity inspired by them, each stretch providing further opportunity for sharpening one's grasp of how best to carry forward with the activity. (Brewer 2009, p. 311)

For these reasons, whilst simple activities may be done mechanically, without thought, but perfectly competently for all that, practices require—for excellence—a sustained quality of attention and focus from the agent.

This description of practices may sound formidably abstract, so let me illustrate what is meant by way of Holt's own favourite example of a practice: that of learning to play a musical instrument. Assuming all goes well, as I engage in this practice my capacities to make music with that instrument improve and expand. A crucial aspect of this expansion is that, as my capacities evolve, the standards I can apply to my own music-making become richer and more sophisticated—things become hearable to me in my own music, which before I had been deaf to. Where once I was concerned with such gross issues as hitting the correct notes and having a regular beat, I find myself now able to judge subtler issues of interpretation—Have I attacked this opening note with appropriate verve? Am I right to play this passage in a stately manner, or does the piece require just a touch of swing to the rhythm? The only way to search for the 'right' interpretation of a musical passage (that is, an interpretation that excels in at least some of the many dimensions of musical excellence) is to play

2.2 Aristotelian Excursus, Part I: Activities

that passage—to engage in the practice—and it is only through engaging with the practice that my capacities in that practice can be deepened and extended. In sum, my grasp of the internal goods of making music on the instrument in question is achieved, dialectically, through the activity of playing itself, and through progressively striving for excellence in that playing.

There are many examples of practices; they are, to use Holt's phrase, what any 'work worth doing and life worth living' will involve. I will not attempt an exhaustive list, but at a minimum they include: all the varied practices of music-making, of dance, and of art; the skilled crafts and trades—working with wood, metal, textiles, and so on; the varied practices of design and architecture; work in medicine and in law; sports and athletics.[2] Crucial to my discussion here is that there are also many varied *practices of inquiry*. There are general forms of this—as it were, the everyday varieties of inquiry we use to find out information, seek explanations, strive for understanding, and so on. And then there are the various highly specialised forms of such inquiry, which we know as disciplines such as chemistry, physics, mathematics, history, philosophy, sociology, and so on and so forth.

I am not claiming that there is a crisp and context-invariant distinction between practices and non-practices (and it is not essential for the purposes of this discussion that there be such a distinction). However, practices are distinguished by their possession of many-dimensioned standards of excellence, and this fact provides us with a rough-and-ready linguistic test for identifying them. We can ask: Can a wide variety of adverbs of excellence be applied to a performance of an activity, or would such application be, in some way, ridiculous, senseless, or absurd? That is, when it comes to the excellent performance of some practice, we can talk about how it was done *rigorously, carefully, imaginatively, creatively, with integrity, diligently*, and so on and so forth (with practices often having, in addition, their own extensive specialised vocabularies for standards of excellence). However, with respect to non-practices, applying such adverbs typically results in absurdity—consider, if you will, the idea of praising some given episode of tooth-brushing or shoe-lace tying with a similar range of adverbs.

2.3 Aristotelian Excursus, Part II: Virtues

Now, this linguistic test in turn points to the fact that the excellent performance of practices is intimately tied to an agent's *character* in a way that the performance of simple activities is not. In order to engage in a practice and reach successfully for its standards of excellence (on a regular basis) one requires certain character traits. Or, to put this another way, an agent who can regularly produce excellent

---

[2]The practice of motorcycle repair deserves an honorable mention here, as it has inspired at least two works of exceptional quality (Pirsig 2004; Crawford 2010), whose themes overlap in various ways with the argument developed here. Two other magnificent books exploring the nature of practices are Sennett (2008) and Sudnow (2001).

examples of a practice thereby possesses certain character traits. Because of this tight logical connection, we often enough use the very same word to characterise both the particular excellence of some engagement in practice, and the character trait of the person who is able to produce such excellence. So, for example, if excellence in some practice demands, let us say, high levels of imagination, creativity, patience, diligence, and attention to detail, then—obviously enough—an excellent practitioner of that practice needs to be (at least with respect to that practice) imaginative, creative, patient, diligent, and attentive to detail.

To use another word for such character traits, these are the *virtues* of the practice in question. As MacIntyre puts it,

> A virtue is an acquired human quality the possession and exercise of which tends to enable us to achieve those goods which are internal to practices and the lack of which effectively prevents us from achieving any such goods. (MacIntyre 1984, p. 191; emphasis removed)

The virtues of a practice are, in part, like a capacity to grasp, or hold steadily in view, the internal goods of a practice (or, equivalently, the internal standards of excellence of that practice). However, the metaphor of vision here is, in some respects, misleading, for it implies that one could 'see' the internal goods of the practice and yet choose not to pursue them. However, having the virtues of the practice entails grasping those internal goods *as goods*—that is, not as ends that 'somebody' could have, but as ends that *I* (the agent) actually have. Furthermore, because those internal goods are only grasped through actually engaging in the practice and aiming at excellence in it (that, after all, is what makes them *internal* goods), the capacity to 'see' the goods is thereby a capacity to engage in the practice in pursuit of them.

The virtues of a given practice thus require, as necessary concomitants, whatever various physical capacities, skills, and knowledge that striving for excellence in that particular practice requires. So, for example, in order to strive for excellence in playing the cello, the agent requires certain capacities for making complex physical movements with arms and fingers, certain auditory capacities, a functioning memory, and so on and so forth; she also requires various skills in reading music, in tuning the instrument, in keeping time, and so on and so forth. However, although such capacities, skills, and knowledge are necessary for striving for excellence in the practice, simply having a 'bundle' of them is not sufficient. It is the possession of the virtues of the practice—or, equivalently, the agent's grasp of the internal goods of that practice—that gives *order*, *unity* and *point* to the exercise of all these varied capacities, skills, and knowledge. Or, to put this another way, the virtues allow us to see the ends, and then deploy the required skills and knowledge appropriately in order to *serve* those ends. That is, it is the agent's active grasp of the standards of excellence of the practice that allow her to determine precisely *how* and *when* such capacities, skills, knowledge need to be drawn on or mobilised. Without the virtues playing this executive, unifying, role, all these capacities, skills, and knowledge are *blind*.

It is Aristotle, in the *Nichomachean Ethics*, who provides what is still the best guide to the conceptual connections that link practices, their internal goods, and the virtues. In that great work, Aristotle's focus is not (as mine is here) on *particular* practices

2.3 Aristotelian Excursus, Part II: Virtues

(such as music, skilled craft, forms of inquiry, etc.), but on what he sees as the practice that overarches and unifies all of them: the practice of living a good (*eudaimon*) life for a human being. The virtues (or, in Aristotle's Greek, *arête*) required for excellence in that overarching practice are the ethical virtues, or what we might call the virtues *simpliciter*, such as courage, temperance, justice and practical wisdom. However, what concerns me here is not these overarching ethical virtues, but the more small-scale virtues of particular practices. The question of how these small-scale virtues relate to the over-arching virtues (for example, how intellectual courage relates to courage *simpliciter*) is an important topic, but beyond the scope of this discussion.

Although the word 'virtue' has the right historical lineage—and is the word used in the philosophical literature on this topic—in everyday English it has unfortunately now a somewhat priggish air about it. However, there is nothing priggish about the particular qualities of character that it encompasses. My focus here—given that this is a discussion about learning and education—is particularly on the virtues of *inquiry*, or what have been termed the *epistemic* or *intellectual* virtues.[3] I have no pretences to offer a systematic typology (nor is it clear what the value of that would be), but these epistemic virtues include such character traits as the following: curiosity, inquisitiveness, reflectiveness, wonder; attentiveness, carefulness, perceptiveness, attention to detail, rigour; fairness, consistency, objectivity, impartiality, fair-mindedness, open-mindedness; honesty, integrity, humility, self-awareness; creativity, imaginativeness, adaptability; determination, patience, courage, resilience, diligence, tenacity (cf. the table given in Baehr 2011, p. 21). Of course, precisely what these virtues come to varies from practice to practice—so that possessing them with regard to one practice of inquiry is no guarantee of possessing them with regard to a different practice. For example, an agent may be highly imaginative in constructing mathematical proofs, but this does not mean that she is therefore imaginative in, say, constructing historical narratives.

So far we have discussed only the virtues of a practice, but opposed to these are also the *vices* of a practice. Put simply, whilst the character traits needed to pursue excellence in a given practice are the virtues required by that practice, the states of character that prevent, or stand in the way of, excellent practice, are the vices of that practice. To put this another way, if the virtues are the capacity, as it were, to keep in view the internal goods of a practice, then the vices are a kind of blindness to those goods. The virtues are thus those character traits in virtue of which the agent is able to resist various temptations that militate against excellence in a practice, and the vices are those character traits in virtue of which the agent is susceptible to those temptations. So, for example, if I possess the virtues of *diligence* and *attention to detail* (in a particular practice) this means, in part, that I am able to resist temptations to be lazy, slapdash, inattentive, or sloppy in performing that practice; to fail to resist such temptations on a regular basis is, precisely, for me to possess the vices of carelessness, laziness, sloppiness, and so forth. Other intellectual vices include such character traits as incuriosity, imperceptiveness, inattention, unfairness, inconsistency, dishonesty,

---

[3] The best discussion of intellectual virtues in the literature is Baehr (2011); see also Roberts and Wood (2007); Hookway (2003).

arrogance, intellectual cowardice, timidity, rigidity, inflexibility, helplessness, passivity, self-distrust, indecisiveness, impatience, unreflectiveness, being unmotivated, self-defeating, etc.

Aristotle famously argues that the ethical virtues are a 'mean' between two vices (the doctrine of the *via media aurea*). The virtues are, that is, 'just the right amount', where either 'too little' or 'too much' results in a characteristic vice. As he puts it,

> it is the nature of such things to be destroyed by defect and excess … For the man who flies from and fears everything and does not stand his ground against anything becomes a coward, and the man who fears nothing at all but goes to meet every danger becomes rash; and similarly, the man who indulges in every pleasure and abstains from none becomes self-indulgent, while the man who shuns every pleasure, as boors do, becomes in a way insensible; temperance and courage, then, are destroyed by excess and defect, and preserved by the mean. (Aristotle 1984, 1104a11–26)

It is possible to mount an argument that the virtues and vices of practices also have this sort of logical structure. For example, paying just the right amount of attention to detail is a virtue, whilst paying too little attention to detail is the vice of *sloppiness*, and paying too much attention to detail is the vice of *obsessionality* or *perfectionism*.

Aristotle's thesis of the 'mean' plays no role in the argument developed here, but it does help to draw attention to a crucially important point: that the virtues of practice involve an indefinitely flexible openness or sensitivity to context. That is, excellence in a practice cannot be reduced to a matter of following explicit rules in an algorithmic fashion. For example, there is no set of precise rules that could be stated such that, following those rules, one would produce an excellent example of a blues song, or a cello concerto, or a piece of abstract art. Thinking of the example from the previous paragraph, how much attention to detail is 'just the right amount'—avoiding either sloppiness (too little) or obsessionality (too much)? Clearly enough, the only general answer that can be given to this is: *it depends* (on the context). This is another way of putting the point that one cannot learn excellence in a practice by learning rules *in abstracto*, but only by engaging in the practice itself, in a way that aims at the internal goods of that practice (even if such goods are, as they always are at first, only dimly or inchoately grasped). Where 'rules' are stated, they can be at most 'rules of thumb' rather than being constitutive of the standards of excellence in the practice. Such rules of thumb are useful in some cases for orienting a beginner towards the internal goods, but learning such rules cannot be a substitute for a vision of those goods.

It is for this reason that Aristotle tells us that the ethical virtues demand practical wisdom (*phronēsis*) in their possessor. He famously defines a virtue as,

> a state concerned with choice, lying in a mean relative to us, this being determined by reason and *in the way in which the person of practical wisdom would determine it*. (1106b36-1107a2; my emphasis)

What is important to note here is how Aristotle does not define ethical choice by appeal to any explicit, stateable, universal rules, but by appeal to how a person of practical wisdom would choose in the particular case. As he writes elsewhere in the *Nichomachean Ethics*, "the agents themselves must in each case consider

2.3 Aristotelian Excursus, Part II: Virtues

what is appropriate to the occasion" (1104a7–8), for "the decision depends upon the particular facts and on perception" (1126b4–5). After all,

> any one can get angry—that is easy—or give or spend money; but to do this to the right person, to the right extent, at the right time, with the right aim, and in the right way, *that* is not for every one. (1109a26–8)

Practical wisdom is precisely the capacity to respond in the right way to the *particulars* of a situation—to know what 'just the right amount' is in a given context. Hence, as G. H. Von Wright remarks,

> virtues have an essential and peculiar connexion with *particulars*. ... *[T]he path of virtue is never laid out in advance*. It is for the man of virtue to determine where it goes in the particular case. (Von Wright 1963, p. 145)

Given this focus on particulars, it is unsurprising that Aristotle compares practical wisdom to a kind of perception—it is, he writes, the "eye of the soul" (1144a29). Similarly, if we are asked for a *general* definition of what constitutes excellence in a practice, we can only reply that it is what excellent practitioners produce. So, the right answer to the question 'What constitutes excellence in jazz?' is to point the asker towards the works of Mingus, Coltrane, Davis, Monk, Marsalis, *et al.*, and say *listen*.

The question that needs to be answered now, is to account for how the virtues of a practice are developed or learned. Here, as before, Aristotle can point us on our way. He writes that,

> The virtues we get by first exercising them, as also happens in the case of the arts (*technê*) as well. For the things we have to learn before we can do, we learn by doing, e.g., men become builders by building and lyre-players by playing the lyre; so too we become just by doing just acts, temperate by doing temperate acts, brave by doing brave acts. (1103a31–1103b2)

We develop the virtues of a practice by engaging in that practice and striving for excellence in it. If things go well for us, that is; for there are no guarantees here. Perhaps we find we simply cannot sustain the sort of focus that excellence in the practice demands, or are unable to develop the particular skills needed to progress further in it. But, with this important caveat noted, the general schema is as follows: We begin with a crude and inchoate view of the internal goods of the practice, and engage in the practice in the light of that view—striving towards the internal standards of excellence of the practice as we see them. If things go well for us, through such striving our view of the internal goods becomes a little clearer, a little more detailed, and hence a little more demanding. And, in doing this, we are engaging in the practice in the way demanded by its virtues, and are thereby developing those virtues—we are, that is, developing the character traits demanded by excellence in that particular practice.

As a way of beginning to draw this account back towards Holt, it is important to emphasise one particular aspect of this account of the virtues of practice. The virtues (and, for that matter, the vices) are related to the agent's *will*. As was pointed out above, the virtues are not the grasp of the internal goods of a practice in some motivation-neutral, 'merely cognitive' sense. Rather, possessing the virtues of a practice means grasping the goods of a practice *as goods*, as something that the agent actually finds worthy of being pursued. Hence, to ascribe a certain virtue to an agent is, in part, to say something about what the agent wants, desires, takes pleasure or joy in—it is to say something about what she loves, is passionate about, finds significant, worthwhile, worth doing, important, and so on. To use the terminology introduced earlier, to ascribe a virtue to an agent is to say something about that agent's evaluative outlook or motivational framework.

This is a crucial respect in which virtues contrast with *skills*. A skill is independent of the will, in that to ascribe a particular skill to an agent says nothing about what that agent wants or desires. A skill is a motivationally-neutral capacity or technique, which the agent can choose to deploy or not, in the service of particular desires that she may have. A virtue, on the other hand, involves the agent having certain desires—namely, desires to strive for the internal goods of the practice in question. As MacIntyre writes,

> To enter into a practice is to accept the authority of those standards and the inadequacy of my own performance as judged by them. It is to subject my own attitudes, choices, preferences and tastes to the standards which currently and partially define the practice. (MacIntyre 1984, p. 190)

Hence, as Aristotle writes, with regard to a skill "he who errs willingly is preferable, but in … the virtues he is the reverse" (1140b23-5). That is, if I make a *deliberate* error in applying a skill, this does not reflect on the level of my skill in the way that my making a genuine (non-deliberate) error would. But in the case of virtues, if I deliberately flout what a virtue requires, then this casts doubt on whether I in fact possess the virtue at all (cf. Foot 2002, pp. 7–8).

To illustrate this point, consider the following example. Suppose that a research scientist omits certain data from a data set, which omission enables her to draw a conclusion (e.g., that a particular herbicide does not cause cancer) that she knows will be looked on favourably by an industry where she has hopes of being employed profitably as a consultant. If, upon this omission being pointed out, she retorts that she omitted that data *deliberately* rather than accidentally, this may well protect her claim to be skilled in data analysis, but it severely undermines any claims she has to possess intellectual virtues such as integrity, honesty, objectivity, impartiality, and rigour. To reiterate, this is because such virtues are not skills (capacities to do certain things successfully), but involve the agent actually *wanting* to strive for certain goods.

As we shall see, this point about the virtues is the insight at the heart of Holt's thought: to grasp what excellence in a practice demands of one is never a 'merely cognitive' achievement. That is, it is not as if the agent could know this, but find this knowledge motivationally inert. Rather, as discussed above, the grasp of the internal goods of a practice is simultaneously cognitive *and* motivational or evaluative. (Or, more accurately, it demonstrates the conceptual crudity of the idea that there is an easy distinction to be had between the 'cognitive' and the 'conative' or motivational.) To put this another way, excellence in an activity requires a passionate attention to the practice—a *love* for what one is doing. In exactly the same way (and as Aristotle discusses at length in the *Nichomachean Ethics*), one cannot know in some 'merely cognitive' way what being a good friend requires of one ('I know what I should do, but I can't really be bothered to do it')—this knowledge must also be passionate. This, as we shall see, is the profound truth of Holt's remark that, "It is not subject matter that makes some learning more valuable than others, but the spirit in which the work is done" (Holt 1982, p. 293). For 'the spirit in which the work is done' is not like icing on a cake—something super-added, which does not change what it overlays—rather, that 'spirit' plays a *constitutive* role in determining the nature of the work done.

2.4 Aristotelian Excursus, Part III: Conclusion

Let me draw some of the threads of this discussion together. I have argued that any engagement in a practice—such as a form of inquiry—is deeply connected to agency, in that such engagement always involves the working of various *character traits* of the agent (whether virtues or vices). And to possess a particular virtue or vice is, in turn, to have a certain sort of *will*. In the case of a virtue, it is to be motivated by certain internal goods, or internal standards of excellence, of the practice in question. Furthermore, because of the dialectical nature of practices, any striving for excellence in a given practice is also simultaneously a transformation of that agent's motivational structure—for the striving results in a progressive revelation of the nature of those internal goods to the agent. In this fashion, striving for excellence in a practice involves a self-transformation—of what the agent values and desires. As MacIntyre writes,

> Individuals discover in the ends of any such practice goods common to all who engage in it, goods internal to and specific to that particular type of practice, which they can make their own only by allowing their participation in the activity to effect a transformation in the desires which they initially brought with them to the activity. (MacIntyre 1994, p. 280)

It is, for example, through striving for excellence in mathematics that the agent transforms herself into a mathematician; it is through striving for excellence in music that the agent transforms herself into a musician. The key point is that such a self-transformation is not simply an acquisition of certain capacities, skills and knowledge, but involves, more fundamentally, a reshaping of the agent's character.

Implied by all this is a fundamental point: if an agent strives for excellence in a practice, then this entails that the agent is engaging in that practice *non-instrumentally*. To engage in an activity instrumentally, is to engage in that activity because it strikes the agent as an efficient and acceptable means to an end or goal that she desires to achieve—where this end or goal is *separate* from the activity. Hence, in the case of instrumental action, if the agent were to come to believe that another activity was a more efficient means to that end, then she would do that instead. Opposed to doing something for instrumental reasons is to engage in an activity non-instrumentally, or *autotelically*. This is to engage in the activity for its own sake.

Any striving for excellence in a practice must, to a significant extent, be autotelic in nature. This is because such striving involves aiming at the internal goods of the practice, and these goods are *internal* precisely in that they can only be embodied in performances of the actual practice in question. Hence, to aim at the internal goods of a practice is to perform the practice for the sake of performing the practice (with excellence)—hence, autotelically.

I will illustrate this important point by extending an example borrowed from *After Virtue* (MacIntyre 1984, pp. 188–9). Chess is a practice, with its own internal goods. The only way to embody those internal goods is in stretches of chess-playing that demonstrate particular virtues (e.g., strategic brilliance, elegance, etc.). Hence, to strive to play excellent chess requires that the player choose to play chess for its own sake. Now, of course our motivations are rarely pure, so our imagined chess-player may also find that chess is, for her, an efficient route to reaching certain ends that she desires—such as money, fame, or status. Clearly enough, chess is not the only way to reach such ends, nor are such ends embodied in stretches of chess-playing. They are, that is to say, *external* goods rather than internal ones. Such goods are related to the practice only contingently, rather than (as internal goods are) playing a constitutive role in making it the practice it is. Our imagined chess-player thus now finds herself engaging in chess both for its own sake, and for the sake of these external goods. So is she engaging in this practice *autotelically* or *instrumentally*? The test will come when these motivations (the autotelic and the instrumental) pull the agent in different directions—as they all too often do. When that occurs, it is the decisions our chess-player makes that will show which motive is dominant in her motivational structure. If the instrumental motivations are dominant then, for example, if she could safely win an important match by cheating then she may well take this option. But if one's primary motivation is play the best chess one can, then cheating is (as MacIntyre remarks) cheating *oneself*.

It is clear enough that the desire for external goods is, all too often, in tension with—or even actively hostile to—the desire for the internal goods of a practice. Capitalism, in particular, often forces a confrontation between them—for in capitalism the only value recognised is exchange value: what something will fetch in the market. So, does one follow the demands of one's craft, or simply produce commercial pap because that is 'what the market wants'? Does one continue to produce pieces of furniture by hand, or simply have cheap knock-offs produced by a factory in a low-wage nation, because that will maximise profit?

At the limit case, however, to 'engage in a practice' from *purely* instrumental reasons is not really to engage in the practice at all. For similar reasons, although I can, of course, struggle for excellence in a practice, yet succeed in producing only rubbish, I cannot engage in a practice with the *deliberate* aim of doing it *badly* (as pointed out in Brewer 2009, pp. 43–5). I have focused above on what is required for striving for excellence in a practice, but *any* kind of engagement with a practice must, to some extent, be motivated by the internal goods, or internal standards of excellence, of that practice. This is because those internal goods are constitutive of the practice being the practice it is. Human action is, after all, such that *which* action is performed by an agent is, in part, constituted by the motivations (desires, intentions)

2.4 Aristotelian Excursus, Part III: Conclusion

that the action proceeds from. (For an act to count as murder, for example, requires that the agent have the intention to murder.) So, suppose, for example, that I engage in something that looks superficially like historical inquiry (in that I read in archives, gather quotations from other historians, etc.). However, suppose further that in doing this I am in fact motivated, *not* by a desire to craft a compelling narrative that is well-grounded in the available historical evidence (an internal good of the practice of history), but purely and entirely by a desire to produce a sensational book that will sell as many copies as possible (an external good). In such a case, there is an important sense in which I am not really engaged in historical inquiry at all—but in a simulacrum of such inquiry. I am, as it were, 'going through the motions' of engaging in historical inquiry, but that is all.

At this point there is a potential objection that needs to be dealt with: this is the suggestion that, contrary to the claims made above, inquiry *is* undertaken instrumentally. After all—the objection runs—the point of engaging in inquiry is to find something out (e.g., the truth of some proposition); and this resulting knowledge is not itself inquiry, but an *external* goal of inquiry. This objection, although tempting, is misguided, because practises of inquiry have a deeper end than merely accumulating states of knowledge. Their goal is an *active* understanding of the world—a doing, rather than a state or capacity (that is, with the word 'understanding' functioning here a gerundive rather than a noun). As Holt puts this point, under the sub-heading "Knowledge is Action,"

> we would do very well to understand that what we have mistakenly come to think of as 'bodies of knowledge' or 'fields of learning' or 'academic disciplines' or 'school subjects' are not nouns but *verbs* … things that people *do*. (Holt 1976, p. 16)

Or, as Brewer puts it,

> The real value of understanding seems to lie in the running actualisation of that understanding itself, both in one's own life and in the lives of others whose view of nature is deepened and extended by one's inquiries. Its value lies in active and self-deepening apprehension of the elegant order of the world in which one's life unfolds. (Brewer 2009, pp. 308–9)

So, the ultimate goal of practices of inquiry is the activity of inquiry itself. For example, the ultimate end of mathematical inquiry is not for the agent to build a collection of states of knowledge (of mathematical truths) and capacities (e.g., the capacity to be able to make use of various proof techniques). These, after all, are mere potentialities. Rather, the end of this practice is the 'running actualisation' of those states and capacities in actual episodes of mathematical understanding—such as solving a mathematical problem, constructing a proof, or working through another's proof. In the same fashion, to take another example, the end of learning music is not to amass a collection of musical knowledge, but to engage in actual episodes of music-making and musical understanding.

This point that practices must, to some extent, be engaged in autotelically, or for their own sakes, illustrates an important point about the nature of motivation. We have seen that there is a crucial difference between undertaking an activity because it is a practice and one is motivated by its internal goods, and undertaking an activity instrumentally, because it is an efficient means for obtaining external goods (such as money, status, or power). That is, motivation, in the sense under discussion here, is not simply a 'force' that is conceptually independent of the activity that it 'sets in motion'. To use an analogy, it not as if activity is like a machine, which can be plugged either into an 'internal' source of power or an 'external' source of power—and so long as it is plugged into one of these, it makes no difference to the operation of the machine. Instead, it is more like the difference between throwing yourself off a cliff, and somebody else throwing you off a cliff. Obviously there is a sense in which the 'falling down the cliff' is the same in each of these, but they are very different 'activities' (one being suicide, and the other murder). To repeat what was said above, the agent's evaluative outlook, or motivational framework, is not simply an impetus to engage in an activity; it plays a constitutive role in, in part, determining *what* that activity is.

2.5 The Best Learning

With these Aristotelian insights into the connections between agency and activity to hand, I now return to begin making sense of those puzzling claims of Holt with which I began this chapter. We saw there that at the heart of Holt's account of learning, and his critique of education, is the claim that there is a kind of learning which is particularly valuable or important. This 'best learning', Holt argues, cannot be produced by undertaking 'learning activities', motivated through external incentives and disincentives. Rather, this 'best learning' is essentially a by-product of activities undertaken by the agent because those activities strike the agent as worth doing in themselves.

As the language just used should already suggest, we can clarify what Holt is talking about here by use of the Aristotelian distinction, introduced above, between engaging in an activity *autotelically*, and engaging in it *instrumentally*. What marks out the activities that make up education, in Holt's sense of the word, is that they are engaged in instrumentally by the agent. That is, the agent views the activity not as worth doing for its own sake, but as an efficient means to an end. The official, external reason for undertaking the activity is to produce certain 'learning outcomes', but of course for many learners—especially those in compulsory schooling—the activity is undertaken because of other sorts of incentives and disincentives (the 'threats' and 'bribes' of which Holt speaks). In either case, the goals or ends of the activity are *external* to the activity, and the activity is an instrument or means for pursuing those ends. In contrast, I suggest, the 'best learning' results from engaging in a practice autotelically—which is to say, in pursuit of what was termed above the *internal* goods of that practice.

In order to fill this picture out, I begin by examining the sort of learning that results from engaging in practices autotelically, and the sense in which that learning is a by-product of the agent's activity. As discussed above, practices have the characteristic of being *dialectical*. This means that, through engaging in the practice, then, if things go well for the agent, her understanding of the standards of excellence that are internal to that practice are deepened and enriched. Or, to put this another way, it is through engaging in the practice that its internal goods progressively reveal themselves to the agent. Consider the following example of this dialectic from Brewer:

> Imagine a singer who is a masterful interpreter of blues songs and who is searching, just now, for the right phrasing and intonation for a key line in a blues number. ... She has no way of discerning what counts as the interpretation she wants except by trying to sharpen her grasp of this goodness she indistinctly perceives, and she may be unable to do this except by attempting to approximate it in song, trusting that she will recognise it when she hears herself sing it. She might sing the line many times over before achieving the interpretation towards which she is drawn. She would then have discovered, or uncovered, what was drawing her all along. (Brewer 2009, p. 47)

There is an important sense in which the singer, in this example, does not know precisely what she is aiming at; that is, she does not begin with a clearly articulated goal, and then devises an efficient route to reach that goal. Rather, the *doing* of the practice is, as Brewer remarks, also a *discovering* or *uncovering* of her goal—of what, precisely, the standards of excellence demand in this particular case. To take another example, it is the same in the practice of writing (e.g., philosophy): one learns just what it is one wants to say *through the activity of writing*—that is, through the difficult work of beginning with a thought that is, at first, grasped only partially, opaquely and inarticulately, and then struggling to bring that thought to clear and precise expression.

It is worth contrasting this sort of dialectical learning with the instrumentalist conception of learning embedded in the very idea of a 'learning outcome' (currently dominant in much educational thinking). A learning outcome is something that can be *precisely specified in advance* of the 'learning activity' being undertaken—it is the future state at which the learning activity aims. To put this another way, a learning activity is intentionally designed to be a means for efficiently bringing about a specified learning outcome in the agent. Paul Hirst, in an early and influential formulation of this sort of approach, argues that this is the *only* effective way of approaching learning. The alternative to treating learning as the efficient pursuit of a fully specified future outcome is, he writes, for learning simply to be "random" (Hirst 1975, p. 170). As he puts it, "Any learning which is not *the learning of some particular X* is as vague as the notion of going somewhere but nowhere in particular" (Hirst 1975, pp. 171–2; my emphasis). But this is simply not true. As we have seen, learning the internal standards of excellence of a practice does not fit this instrumentalist picture. It is not that the agent engaged in a struggle for excellence in a practice knows exactly where she is going, and then works out an efficient route to get to that location. Rather, as in the example of the blues singer, the finding out where she is going is identical to the activity of getting there. The blues singer does not begin with a grasp of a clearly articulated future state of affairs, at which her efforts then aim (if she did have that grasp, then her search would be over). In the absence of that grasp, is she therefore, as Hirst would have us say, floundering vaguely about, 'going nowhere in particular'? Of course not, and Hirst can only write this because he has nourished his thinking with a one-sided diet of examples.[4]

In dialectical learning, like that of Brewer's blues singer, it needs to be emphasised that, whilst the agent is aiming at achieving excellence in a *particular* case, if all goes well she thereby learns things that enable her to reach for higher standards of excellence that reach *beyond* that particular case. That is, discovering what the internal standards of excellence of a practice demand in a particular case, is also a discovery of what they demand more generally; the discovery that is made in the particular case further illuminates, for the agent, the practice as a whole. Let me explain this important point further. As discussed, the only way to strive for excellence in a practice, is to actually engage in the practice itself. And this means striving for excellence in a *particular* episode of undertaking the activity—in the example above, it means *this* singing, *here* and *now*. Yet this struggle for excellence here and now is how the agent comes to a deeper grasp of the internal goods of the practice—goods that reach right across the practice, and do not pertain simply to this particular case. That is, it is only through struggling for excellence in particular cases that the agent transforms herself into someone who understands what excellence demands across the practice.

As discussed above, the agent's growing understanding of the internal goods of a practice just *is* the agent's development of the virtues of the practice. So, how does our imagined agent become an excellent singer of the blues? Only by striving for excellence with *this* piece on *this* occasion, and *that* piece on *that* occasion, and so on. Yet it is through all these particular episodes of striving that the agent transforms herself (if all goes well) into someone who comes to possess the general virtues of that musical practice, and can thus reach higher levels of excellence across the practice (not just in those particular cases). In sum, it is through doing the practice for its own sake, that the internal goods of the practice are progressively grasped by, revealed to, the agent; and this, in turn, just is for the agent to further develop the virtues of the practice.

Compare this to the remark from Aristotle quoted above, that "we become just by doing just acts, temperate by doing temperate acts, brave by doing brave acts" (1103a35–1103b2). By this, as Burnyeat remarks, "Aristotle is not simply giving us a bland reminder that virtue takes practice. Rather, practice has cognitive powers, in that *it is the way we learn what is noble or just*" (Burnyeat 1980, p. 73; my emphasis). That is, it is *only* through particular strivings for excellence (trying to do the right thing in *this* situation, and *that* situation, etc.) that we learn 'what is noble or just'. This is because 'what is noble or just' cannot be embodied in the form of a collection of universal rules. If it could be summed up in a collection of rules, then we could learn 'what is noble or just' simply by learning those rules *in abstracto*, without engaging in the actual practice. But, as we have seen, to do 'what is noble or just' requires responding to the *particulars* of each case, "to the right extent, at

---

[4]"A main cause of philosophical disease—a one-sided diet: one nourishes one's thinking with only one kind of example" (Wittgenstein 1958, §593).

2.5 The Best Learning

the right time, with the right aim, and in the right way" (as Aristotle puts it). Hence, this learning must of necessity be embodied in the agent's developing virtues.

What we have here, then, is learning—the development of the virtues of the practice in question—that is essentially a by-product of engaging in that practice autotelically, or for its own sake. This is to say, this learning *cannot* be aimed at directly or intentionally; to do so is self-defeating. This is because the virtues of the practice are acquired only by engaging in the practice in pursuit of its internal goods. Given that those internal goods can only be embodied in particular stretches of the practice (that is, after all, the sense in which they are 'internal'), to engage in the practice in pursuit of them, is to engage in the practice for its own sake.

Consider again the imagined blues singer discussed above. To strive for excellence in this particular undertaking of the practice, is for the agent to have as her primary aim: *Getting this song right*. She is not, for example, engaging in the practice with the primary aim of: *Becoming a great blues singer*. (Indeed, engaging in the practice with that kind of aim as primary is a route to acquiring the musical vices that stem from narcissism: self-indulgence, flashiness, cheapness, and the like.) Nor, for that matter, is she engaging in the practice with a view to improving certain technical skills. To do this would be to treat the song as an exercise—as simply a means to an end—and not as worth 'getting right' for its own sake. That is, it would entail that the primary focus of her desires is not performing this particular song with excellence, here and now, but rather the *future* state of having certain improved technical capacities. Hence, the quality of the learning that the agent derives from this activity comes from the fact that this activity is *not* engaged in to produce learning. Instead, the quality comes from the fact that the practice is illuminated by the agent's desires to *get this song right*. If the agent's primary motivation were instead the acquisition of certain character traits, or simply to improve certain skills, then *ipso facto* this would imply that 'getting this right' would lack the appropriate level of significance and value for that agent—and thus the learning would not occur.

To put this another way, the learning that is a progressive deepening of one's grasp of the internal goods of a practice, can come about only through engaging in the practice with a certain quality of attention (to what one is doing)—an intensity of attention that we can call *love*. To have this love for what one is doing, is for one's evaluative outlook to make the internal goods of the practice the primary focus of significance or value during one's doing of that activity—so that in engaging in the practice, one is attending and responding to the demands of those internal goods. This is for those internal goods to be, from the perspective of the agent, the pre-eminent reasons *why* she is engaged in the practice at that moment in time. In contrast, insofar as the agent views the activity mainly as an efficient means to an end—even if that end is *to learn certain things*—then that agent lacks the motivational structure required to achieve that deepened grasp of the internal goods of the practice. Hence, the acquisition of the virtues of a practice are essentially a by-product of engagement in that practice, for such learning can occur only if the practice is engaged in autotelically (for its own sake), rather than instrumentally.

The logic of this argument is precisely the same as Aristotle's point about the conceptual impossibility of acquiring the ethical virtues via instrumental action.

Suppose I undertake actions that, to external observers, appear brave; however, from the first-person perspective, I am undertaking these actions because they appear to me as efficient means to the end of producing a certain impression on observers—that they think of me as brave, and hence accord me a certain status. To undertake actions instrumentally like this (in pursuit of the public *appearance* of bravery) will not result in me developing the virtue of bravery. For a constitutive part of having that virtue is that I desire to do brave acts simply because they are the right (or excellent) thing to do in this particular set of circumstances. That is, part of having the virtue of bravery is to have an evaluative outlook in which brave acts are worth doing *for their own sake* (and thus independently of whatever impression they may or may not make on observers).

We now have an answer to our question of what Holt is talking about when he talks of the best, most valuable, important, or 'true' learning. This 'best learning' is *the agent's development of the virtues of a practice*. This is what is required for the agent to engage in a given practice to a higher level of excellence. Of course such development entails a growth in the usual objects of learning—in the various skills, technical capacities, and knowledge required for such higher levels of excellence. However, it *also* entails that the agent has a growing grasp of the internal goods, or internal standards of excellence, of that practice, and what they demand in particular circumstances. And, as we have seen, this is just another way of saying that such learning involves the development of the agent's character. This learning is essentially a by-product of the agent's engagement in a practice for its own sake (autotelically); it cannot be produced by engaging in the practice simply as an efficient means to some external end (instrumentally). This is because possessing the virtues of a practice entails that the agent possesses an evaluative outlook which focuses on the internal goods of the practice as the primary reason for engaging in the practice. This, in turn, means that the agent brings a particular quality of attention to her engagement in the practice: she engages in the practice with *love*. Hence (to repeat Holt's words, quoted above), "It is not subject matter that makes some learning more valuable than others, but the spirit in which the work is done" (Holt 1983, p. 293).

This conclusion also explains Holt's repeated claim that we can achieve this 'best learning' *only by doing*: "We learn to do something by doing it. There is no other way" (Holt 1976, p. 13). Holt's claim runs precisely parallel to Aristotle's remark that we can become brave only by doing brave acts. As discussed above, the internal standards of excellence of a practice cannot be formulated as rules. If they could be, then these rules could be learned *in abstracto*, without actual engagement in the practice. However, as argued, to strive towards excellence in a practice requires learning to respond appropriately to the particulars of the context—that is, through developing the virtues of the practice. And this learning can only be achieved by engaging in the practice itself.

I am now in a position to provide a clearer account of Holt's critique of education. Stated in summary form, it is this: *in education, practices tend to be engaged in by agents out of instrumental motivations; education thereby tends to be hostile to the development of the virtues of practices*. We have already remarked that instrumentalism is pervasive in educational institutions: most learners undertake the 'learning

2.5 The Best Learning

activities' within such institutions, not because they find those activities intrinsically valuable, but because of the motivation provided by external incentives and disincentives. In turn, this instrumentalism means, for the reasons explored above, that educational activities tend to be hostile to the agent's development of the virtues of practices. Viewing an activity as worth doing for instrumental reasons, is to value that activity primarily as an efficient means to producing a certain end—where that end is something external to the doing of the practice. From this evaluative outlook, what will be worth doing is whatever will appear to the agent as most efficiently achieving that external end—rather than what will best meet, in the particular case, the practice's own standards of excellence. To put this another way, the more the practice is approached instrumentally, the less the agent's evaluative outlook illuminates the internal goods of the practice. Hence, the less the agent will be able to develop a deepening grasp of those internal goods; or, equivalently, the less the agent will be able to develop the virtues of the practice.

2.6 Unity and Fragmentation

There is an important objection to this analysis of instrumentalism and its hostility to the virtues of practices, which Holt discusses and rejects in various places in his works. This objection runs as follows—and I will follow Holt's approach in taking the practice of music-making as my example, although it could be extended to any practice:

> In becoming a musician, much time and effort is typically spent on playing scales, arpeggios, and various other exercises. Surely—so the objection runs—these activities are approached instrumentally, rather than being done for their own sakes. That is, they are done purely as an efficient means to produce a future learning outcome (the development of certain facility of technique). If this is the case, then there is a legitimate place within practices for instrumentally motivated activity.

This imagined objection thus divides the practice of music-making into two parts: the 'playing', which is done for its own sake, and a part consisting of various exercises, which are done as efficient means to particular ends. This in turn suggests, contrary to the argument developed above, that one can, at least in part, develop the virtues of musicianship via instrumental means.

Holt responds to this objection at some length in a number of works, and a brief exploration of his response will show how the analytic framework developed in this chapter makes good sense of what he is saying. In *Instead of Education*, Holt writes of,

> the strange idea that there exist two different processes: (1) learning to play the cello; and (2) playing the cello. … Of course, this is nonsense. There are not two processes, but one. We learn to do something by doing it. There is no other way. (Holt 1976, p. 13)

In his posthumously published work, *Learning All the Time*, he writes that,

> A father once told me that his daughter likes to play the violin, but hates to practice. Why talk about 'practice'? Why not just talk about playing the violin? ... What do I do with my cello? I *play*. I don't spend part of my time getting ready to play it, and the rest of the time playing it. Some of the time I play scales or things like that; some of the time I play pieces that I am going to play with other people; some of the time I read new music; some of the time I improvise. But all the time I am playing the cello. ... For me there is no such thing as 'practice'. (Holt 1989, p. 111)

And in an extended discussion of this same topic in *Freedom and Beyond*, he writes that,

> for someone who really loves playing an instrument, scales are part of that playing. ... I don't divide my practice into pleasant and unpleasant parts, and then use 'will-power' to make myself do the unpleasant ones so that I may later have the fun of doing the pleasant. It is all one. (Holt 1972, p. 113)

Splitting 'practice' (as in, scales and other exercises) off from 'playing'—or, more generally, separating *learning* from *doing*—tends to makes the former activity unpleasant, or burdensome, for the agent. This is because to treat an activity as learning is to treat it instrumentally—as an efficient means to produce some 'learning outcome'—rather than autotelically. And this is for the agent to undertake that activity with an evaluative outlook that is focused on the activity's expected future outcome rather the present doing. This in turn tends to damage the agent's approach to the whole of music-making.

Holt's response to this, as the quotes above show, is that the agent needs to avoid such splitting, and instead keep steadily in view the unity of the practice of music-making—as a unified *doing*. Hence, he writes that, when he found himself desiring to sleep in on a cold morning and avoid his cello playing,

> my response to this [desire] was not to draw on something called willpower, to insult or threaten myself, but to take a longer look at my life to extend my vision, to think about the whole of my experience, to reconnect present and future ... If, as sometimes happened or happens, I do stay in bed ... it is not because will-power is weak but because I have temporarily become disconnected, so to speak, from the wholeness of my life. (Holt 1972, p. 113)

What Holt is pointing to here, is that approaching an activity in instrumental terms *fragments* that activity. I perform task #1 to achieve goal #1; I then perform task #2 to achieve goal #2; and so on—where each of these tasks and goals are conceptually independent, or external to one another. In contrast, engaging autotelically in a practice is for the agent's activity to make up a unified whole (cf. Brewer 2009, Chap. 2). Whilst the activities that make up the practice may be many and varied—in the case of music-making, consist of playing whole pieces, fragments of pieces, exercises, scales, and so forth—they are all parts of a unitary, on-going attempt to grasp and articulate the internal goods of the practice. Or consider a different example: suppose the agent undertakes a certain form of inquiry (e.g., seeking an historical understanding of some past event). In this case, the agent will undertake a variety of activities—research in primary and secondary sources, reading, writing, interpreting, analysing, and so on. However, all of these varied activities will be bound together

2.6 Unity and Fragmentation

into a unity: they are all parts of an ongoing articulating of an historical understanding, where this articulating is at the same time a discovering or uncovering of just what the internal goods of historical inquiry demand of this understanding. Thus—to return to Holt's example of music-making—to maintain the quality of attention and love that striving for excellence in the practice demands, the agent should not view the playing of scales and exercises instrumentally, as efficient means to some future end. Rather, the agent should view them as components of a unified practice of music-making, the whole of which is animated by the agent's on-going attempt to reach for, and further articulate, the internal goods of that practice. As the great jazz trumpeter Wynton Marsalis remarks, "Treat *everything* you play on your instrument as an important piece of music, even if you are just warming up" (Marsalis 1995, p. 130; cf. Green 1986).

The thought that education—the instrumentalising of activity, in separating 'learning' from 'doing'—fragments the unity of human practices, is a theme to which Holt regularly returns. Such talk of fragmentation or 'splitting' is another way of putting the point that such instrumental activity is hostile to the development of the virtues of the practice. To recall what was discussed above, excellence in a practice involves the deployment of knowledge, skills and capacities of various kinds. However, the executive centre, so to speak, of this deployment is the virtues of that practice. For it is the agent's possession of the virtues of the practice—or, equivalently, the agent's grasp of the internal goods of the practice—that allow her to deploy the knowledge, skills, and capacities in just the way called for by the particulars of the situation. To put this another way, it is the possession of the virtues of the practice that give a *unity* to all the variety of knowledge, skills and capacities required by the practice—through which their deployment coheres in a meaningful way, as a unified pursuit of the internal goods of the practice.

In contrast, while instrumental activity can, of course, result in the learning of various rules, techniques, skills, knowledge, and so on, what cannot be learned this way is the unity of a practice. For, as we have seen, this unity comes from the agent's developing grasp of the internal goods of the practice—and this, in turn, comes only through pursuing the practice for its own sake. Treated instrumentally, a practice is fragmented into a mere collection or bundle of skills and pieces of knowledge. This is a mere 'bundle', rather than a genuine unity, in that it lacks the overall coherence given to their deployment by the agent's grasp of the internal goods of the practice. Without such a grasp, the agent may, for example, know *that* such-and-such is the case, and she may know *how* to do such-and-such, but she cannot reliably deploy those capacities in the ways demanded by the practice's internal standards of excellence. In contrast, learning these under the aegis of the practice's virtues makes a unified, coherent whole out of these skills, knowledge and capacities. That is, the 'best learning' involves the agent not just learning certain skills, knowledge, and capacities, but—most importantly—also developing a growing sense of what it is to deploy them (to quote Aristotle's words again), "to the right extent, at the right time, with the right aim, and in the right way".

2.7 How Children Fail

Holt's first book, *How Children Fail*, is a detailed narrative exploration of what happens when children learn instrumentally, and hence in a fragmented way—in the absence of any real grasp of the internal goods of a practice. Through the use of ethnographic-like techniques of close observation, and the detailed recording of children's conversations, Holt is able to move away from the all-too-familiar teacher's perspective on a class, and let us come closer to seeing educational activities from the students' perspective. What we see from this agent's perspective are children who lack, to a striking degree, any real grasp of the internal goods of the practices of inquiry that they are nominally engaged in. These are, as Holt notes, 'good' students at a 'good' school—and as such, the children have some relevant knowledge, and possess various skills and techniques in inquiry. However, what they lack is the capacity to deploy the knowledge and skills they possess, in the way that the internal standards of the practice demand in the particular context. They cannot, that is, deploy what knowledge and skills they do possess "to the right extent, at the right time, with the right aim, and in the right way".

To put this another way, what we see again and again in Holt's narratives, are children who are entirely missing the overall *point* or *meaning* of the inquiry that is nominally underway. They make use of rules and techniques in a manner that is mechanical, and done without any sense of when such uses are appropriate (that is, when they assist in reaching for the internal goals of the inquiry). Rules of thumb —useful in some contexts—are used without appropriate judgment, and treated as invariant and constitutive. That is, they are used with no grasp of the internal goods that the rules are an attempt to express. In some cases there are children who are able to "crank out right answers", but "without the faintest idea of what they were doing" (Holt 1982, p. 176). Overall, through the narratives of *How Children Fail*, we see that what should be a unitary, coherent, developing inquiry is, from these children's perspective, seen as a series of separate, disconnected activities—strung together without rhyme or reason. It is thus unsurprising that, as Holt shows in detail, the children perform these activities in the manner of people performing the rites of a long dead religion, with no grasp of what they are really doing, or why.

At the limit, as external (instrumental) motivations come to overwhelm the children's evaluative outlook on their own activity, we see from Holt's account just what we would expect: that the children are not really engaged in practices of inquiry at all. Rather, the instrumental motivation results in them engaging in something that just has the *appearance* of inquiry. The main external motivation that Holt points to is *fear*—fear of the consequences of giving a wrong answer, such as the resulting public humiliation (e.g., mockery from one's peers), or of disappointing the teacher's expectations, or of disappointing the children's own expectations of themselves. When a child's evaluative outlook is dominated by an external end like fear, the result is a choice of strategies which bear no relation at all to the internal goods of the practice of inquiry in which the child is nominally engaged. As Holt documents, fear results in such strategies as 'fence-sitting' or 'hedging one's bets' (i.e., avoiding commitment to an answer); attempting to 'read' the teacher for the answer; attempts to manipulate the teacher into providing the answer. From an instrumental perspective, these strategies make perfectly good sense: they appear as efficient means to the end of 'avoiding a wrong answer'. But for an agent engaged in an inquiry for its own sake (i.e., because it appears interesting, worth while, valuable, etc.) these strategies would make no sense at all. In other words, what Holt shows us is that, although the children may, to a superficial external observation, be engaged in what looks like mathematics or some other form of inquiry, by paying close attention to what they say and do, it becomes obvious that they are in fact *not doing this at all*—they are, instead, engaged in a simulacrum of such inquiries. As discussed above, a practice cannot be pursued instrumentally (i.e., in a way dominated by external ends), because a practice is constituted by its *internal* goods. Yet external ends—external incentives and disincentives; 'bribes' and 'threats'—are precisely how motivation is typically provided in school. Hence, as Holt writes,

> these children see school almost entirely of the day-to-day and hour-to-hour tasks that we impose on them. … For children, the central business of the school is not learning … it is getting these daily tasks done, or at least out of the way, with a minimum of effort and unpleasantness. (Holt 1982, pp. 37–8)

After all, he suggests, from the students' perspective it certainly looks like "what most teachers want and reward are not knowledge and understanding but the appearance of them" (Holt 1982, p. 255).

At this point, it is worth pausing briefly to clarify the epistemological status of the narratives in *How Children Fail*. As noted in the previous chapter, Holt deliberately avoids what I termed there the 'scholarly mode of telling', and tends to argue his case via a web of narratives. As remarked, this form of writing leaves him open to the charge of being a retailer of 'mere anecdotes', and thereby failing to establish his position with sufficient empirical rigour. However, as can seen from the discussion above, this objection misunderstands what Holt is doing. The objection assumes that Holt is making *empirical* claims, and then providing 'anecdotes' as second-rate evidence for those claims—rather than, say, data derived from systematic surveys. But Holt is pointing out (among other things) that children whose evaluative outlook is dominated by an external end like fear, do not engage in genuine inquiry. As I have argued here, this is not an empirical claim but a conceptual one—it concerns the logical connections between the concepts of a *practice of inquiry*, *agency*, and *autotelic* versus *instrumental* activity. Holt's narratives are an attempt to make these conceptual connections—which I have discussed in this chapter in an abstract fashion—living and concrete for the reader. To put this another way, Holt's narratives function, to use a Wittgensteinian phrase, not as patchy, second-rate empirical evidence, but as *reminders* of conceptual connections to which we have not given due weight in our thoughts and practices. The doings of Nell, Emily, Martha, Nancy, Sam, Nat, and the rest, that Holt discusses in *How Children Fail* are real, but they need not have been; in an important sense, Holt is giving us parables that aim to illuminate the nature of learning.

2.8 Drawing Together the Threads

I have argued that Holt's notion of the 'best learning' is the agent's development of the virtues of a practice, through striving for excellence in that practice. Such activity entails that the agent engage with the practice in pursuit of its internal goods, or standards of excellence; hence, it entails that the agent undertake the practice autotelically, or for its own sake. This means that the 'best learning' is essentially a by-product of activity undertaken because it strikes the agent as significant, valuable, or worth doing in its own right. Such activity is, in Holt's phrase, genuine "*doing*—self-directed, purposeful, meaningful life and work"; or, as I have put it, it is engaging in human practices with passionate attention.

Another way that Holt expresses this thought is with his repeated slogans that 'living is learning' and that 'learning is an expansion of the self'. In *What Do I Do Monday*, for example, he writes that,

> we can best understand learning as growth, an expanding of ourselves into the world around us. We can also see that there is no difference between living and learning, that living *is* learning, that it is impossible, and misleading, and harmful to think of them as separate. (Holt 1970, p. 23)

Living is learning, because it is through 'work worth doing' that the best kind of learning takes place—the learning that is a deepening and articulating of the internal goods of practices, rather than the fragmented grasping of skills and pieces of knowledge, lacking a coherent unity and point. The best *learning*, in other words, is one and the same as the best *doing*—autotelic activity—which is, for both Aristotle and Holt, a key component of the good life for a human being.

In turn, such learning is an expansion of the self—that is, of *agency*. This is because the learning that is the acquisition of the virtues of practice is not simply a learning of skills, knowledge and capacities (although it does entail such learning). Rather, it is a transformation, or reshaping, of the agent's character—of what is desired, wanted, found valuable, significant. For as one comes to comprehend the internal goods of a practice, so one's desires for those goods become deeper and more articulate. In other words, through engagement in a practice, one does not simply develop capacities to be able to do more; it is also the case that what one wants, desires, values, and intends becomes richer and more extensive. In this way, one's agency is now expressed through that practice in a way it was not before.

Consider, for example, what happens as an agent develops as a musician. She finds that the instrument (which before had seemed like an *obstacle* to action; something alien to the self) slowly becomes a part of herself, through which she can express her desires and what she values and finds significant. Or consider an agent developing as a mathematician: she can now possess desires that are articulable *only* in mathematics (the desire to achieve a certain elegance in a particular proof, for example) and the mathematical techniques she has mastered become available modes of expression for articulating such desires. In each case, through the striving for excellence in a practice, an aspect of the world—musical forms; mathematical structures—becomes

2.8 Drawing Together the Threads

available to the learner, as a domain in which her agency is expressed. It seems natural to call this, as Holt does, an 'expansion of the self into the world'.

To learning as a by-product of genuine 'doing', Holt opposes 'education'. As he uses this term, it involves undertaking activities which are intended as a means of producing certain learning outcomes. That is, educational activities are not intended to be worth doing for their own sakes, but for the sake of the valued future outcome that they are intended to accomplish. In a word, education (in Holt's sense) is *instrumental* activity. It is thus "learning cut off from active life"—learning that has been separated from activity that is significant to an agent for its own sake.

Holt's consistent emphasis on the importance of the learner's freedom and autonomy follows as an obvious corollary of this view. To produce 'best learning' requires the agent to undertake activity autotelically; that is, because the activity strikes the agent as worth doing for its own sake. If a learner is *only* engaging in an activity because she is coerced or manipulated into doing so—through 'bribe' or 'threat'—then this necessarily renders the agent's activity instrumental rather than autotelic. After all, to coerce or manipulate somebody is to motivate that agent through the use of *external* goods—so that an activity shows up for that agent as worth doing because it is an efficient means of obtaining a valued thing (e.g., a proffered reward), or avoiding a bad thing (e.g., a threatened punishment). But autotelic activity is for the agent to be primarily motivated by the *internal* goods of a practice—and that means that the agent would undertake that activity in the absence of any external motivation. Hence, the absence of freedom for a learner—that is, a coercive or manipulative educational environment (such as found in compulsory schooling)—is intrinsically hostile to autotelic activity, and therefore hostile to the acquisition of the virtues of practices.

It should be noted that this is not to claim that autotelic activity is *impossible* in a coercive context. It is perfectly possible—indeed, it is an everyday occurrence—for an agent to begin working at a practice in pursuit of external goods, and then slowly come to grasp the internal goods of the practice. For example, a student who was compelled to undertake an activity may come to value a practice for its own sake—for example, because a teacher, or reading the right book at the right time, succeeds in opening her eyes to its worth. Similarly, a child may begin playing a musical instrument in order to please his parents (another example of an external incentive), but come to love the music-making for its own sake. However, what has occurred in such cases is not that autotelic activity has been brought about by the influence of external incentives or disincentives. Rather, what has occurred is a *transformation* in the agent's desires, and how she sees and values the activity. This has occurred *in spite of* the presence of external (instrumental) motivations, rather than *because of* them. External motivations necessarily cannot produce autotelic engagement. Indeed, the more oppressive, or compelling, the external reasons appear to the agent, the less likely it is for that agent to be able to 'look past' such motivations, to grasp the internal goods of a practice.

In this way, in virtue of its instrumentalist tendencies, education—and this is truer, the greater its reliance on external motivators (i.e., the more coercive or manipulative it is)—tends to undermine the pursuit of excellence in practices, and thereby tends to undermine agents' acquisition of the virtues of those practices. In other words, education is intrinsically hostile to agents engaging in practices with the kind of quality of attention, or love for what they are doing, that is required for the 'best learning'. Compulsory schooling is an obvious example of a highly coercive framework—and one which was Holt's focus—but such coercion can come in more subtle ways. For example, whilst university study is not compulsory, and thus lacks the legal coercion that forms the framework of more junior levels of schooling, it is nonetheless the case that, as remarked in the previous chapter, in many countries a university qualification has become more and more essential for access to decent work. This credentialism is a powerful external motivator for students, and it is easy to see that it is hostile to a student's pursuit of a practice for its own sake. After all, if one's primary motivation is to obtain a credential perceived as necessary to a decent standard of living, then, for example, plagiarism, exam cheating, or the use of essay mills, may well appear to the agent as an efficient means to that end (and certainly appears that way to many students). But if one is undertaking a practice of inquiry for its own sake, then such cheating makes no sense at all.

Holt's critique of education as instrumentalised learning can be seen as a radicalisation of the well-known concept of the 'hidden curriculum'. The hidden curriculum is the idea that compulsory schooling does not communicate simply the content of its official, explicit curriculum (numeracy, literacy, and so on) to its students. Rather, it also implicitly communicates certain ideas in virtue of its bureaucratic, authoritarian form—such as epistemological ideas about the nature of knowledge and the knowing self; political ideas about individualism and competitiveness. All of these are implicitly 'taught' by school's organisation, hierarchy, and procedures (cf. Barrow 1978, pp. 136–9.) Holt's critique of education can be seen as radically extending this idea by criticising the impact of the *instrumentalist* form that education tends overwhelmingly to take in our culture, and how this impacts the evaluative outlook that learners bring to their own activity.

2.9 Stupidity and Intelligence

Making use of the Aristotelian analysis developed earlier in the chapter, I have discussed Holt's claims that the 'best learning' is essentially a by-product of practices engaged in for their own sake, and that the instrumental motivations characteristic of educational practice are hostile to such learning. Of the claims we began the chapter with, there is one more that needs explanation and clarification. This is Holt's claim that education has an intrinsic tendency to be damaging to the agent *qua* inquirer. Or, in his own flamboyantly counter-intuitive words, "To a very large degree, school is a place where children learn to be stupid" (Holt 1982, p. 263).

Stated in the terms used here, this latter claim is that engaging instrumentally in a practice not only prevents the acquisition of the virtues of a practice, but is in fact conducive to developing the *vices* of the practice. The vices of a practice, after all, are those character traits in virtue of which an agent is susceptible to the temptations that militate against excellence in that practice. Approaching a practice instrumentally tends to encourage an agent to give into such temptations. To begin with, the more instrumental the agent's perspective, the more she is focussed on the anticipated *future* outcomes of the activity, rather than on her *present* activity. Instrumentalism, in other words, is hostile to the quality of attention—the *love* for the activity—that excellence demands. Furthermore, as has been remarked on above, external motives will not pull in the same direction as the internal goods of the practice, and are often in direct opposition to them. Hence, an agent with an instrumental focus will feel strong temptations to perform the practice in a way that fails to meet its internal standards of excellence. For these reasons, then, instrumental motivations—those external incentives and disincentives characteristic of typical educational contexts—are an encouragement to acquiring the vices of a practice.

When we focus on practices of *inquiry*, then possession of the vices of those practices is precisely what Holt means by 'stupidity'. Consider Holt's discussion of intelligence versus stupidity in the conclusion of *How Children Fail*, a passage which is worth quoting at some length.

> When we talk about intelligence, we do not mean the ability to get a good score on a certain kind of test, or even the ability to do well in school; these are at best only indicators of something larger, deeper, and far more important. By intelligence we mean a style of life, a way of behaving in various situations, and particularly in new, strange, and perplexing situations. The true test of intelligence is not how much we know how to do, but how we behave when we don't know what to do.
>
> The intelligent person, young or old, meeting a new situation or problem ... grapples with it boldly, imaginatively, resourcefully, and if not confidently at least hopefully; if he fails to master it, he looks without shame or fear at his mistakes and learns from them. This is intelligence. ...
>
> The bright child is curious about life and reality, eager to get in touch with it, embrace it ... The bright child is patient. He can tolerate uncertainty and failure, and will keep trying until he gets an answer. ... Not so the dull child. He cannot stand uncertainty or failure. To him, an unanswered question is not a challenge or an opportunity, but a threat.
>
> The bright child is willing to go ahead on the basis of incomplete understanding and information. He will take risks ... But the dull child will go ahead only when he thinks he knows exactly where he stands and exactly what is ahead of him. (Holt 1982, pp. 271–3)

In this passage, Holt's distinction between the 'bright child' and the 'dull child' is framed entirely—to use the Aristotelian terminology of this chapter—in terms of possession of the virtues and vices of inquiry: the character traits that make people good inquirers or bad inquirers. The bright child, that is, is a person who possesses the virtues of inquiry to a high degree: intellectual courage, curiosity, imaginativeness, resourcefulness, hopefulness, and so on. The dull child, on the other hand, is someone who possesses the vices of inquiry to a high degree: lack of imagination, passivity, helplessness, intellectual cowardice, self-distrust, and so on. Similarly, consider Holt's summation in *Teach Your Own* of what the 'best learning' is concerned with: "What makes people smart, curious, alert, observant, competent, confident, resourceful, persistent—in the broadest and best sense, intelligent" (p. 235). What is this characterisation of intelligence ('in the broadest and best sense') but a list of the key virtues of inquiry?

Holt thus offers us an account of intelligence (and hence, stupidity) in terms of the agent's possession, or lack, of the virtues of inquiry. It is worth bringing out what is distinctive about this view, by briefly contrasting it with a more standard modern account. Consider Ledger Wood's definition:

> Intelligence is the capacity of the mind to meet effectively—through the employment of memory, imagination, and conceptual thinking—the practical and theoretical problems with which it is confronted. (Wood 1963, p. 147)

A number of issues could be raised with this definition, such as the intellectualist presuppositions contained in the word 'mind', but the key issue lies in the bland phrase 'problems with which it is confronted'. This is a conception of intelligence as a General Problem Solver, where it is irrelevant whether those problems are humanly significant or trivial. It is, in other words, a strongly *instrumentalist* account of intelligence—of intelligence not as involving the grasping of ends, but simply as a calculator of efficient means.

What this helps to bring out is that, in important ways, calling something 'intelligent' is praise, so there is no ethically neutral definition of it to be had. That is, any account of intelligence will, implicitly or explicitly, build in some conception of the human good; some conception of the kinds of activities that are considered valuable, important, and significant. Hence, it is unsurprising that a civilisation like ours, that focuses on instrumental uses of reason to the exclusion of the autotelic, will tend to think of intelligence as a kind of raw 'problem solving' capacity—focused on the efficient reaching of goals. Thus, for example, the attention given to IQ testing, which focuses on the agent's capacity to manipulate abstractions in highly decontextualized ways. In contrast, Holt, like Aristotle, sees the human good as lying in 'work worth doing': in rich human practices, done for their own sake, with passionate attention to the particulars of the context, and a striving to meet the practice's internal standards of excellence. To engage in practices of inquiry in this way, demands that the agent possess the virtues of inquiry.

Holt's argument thus leads to the conclusion that education—thanks to its tendency to rely on external incentives and disincentives—systematically encourages learners to develop the vices of understanding. That is, as he puts it, school tends to make students stupid. As we have seen, striving for excellence (and hence the development of the virtues of a practice) involves a continuous attention to the internal goods of that practice. Engaging in an activity out of instrumental motivations, however, is hostile to this sort of loving attention. As Holt writes,

> Give a child the kind of task he gets in school, and whether he is afraid of it, or resists it, or is willing to do but bored by it, he will do the task with only a small part of his attention, energy, and intelligence. In a word, he will do it stupidly—even if correctly. (Holt 1982, pp. 263–4)

In contrast,

> A child is most intelligent when the reality before him arouses in him a high degree of attention, interest, concentration, involvement—in short, when he cares most about what he is doing. (Holt 1982, p. 265)

2.9 Stupidity and Intelligence

As we have seen, when we are dealing with practices of inquiry (rather than simple, mechanical tasks), the *way* in which an activity is done by an agent makes all the difference in the world. We can imagine two students in school, who are engaged in the same kind of inquiry and—in an 'external' sense—are both 'doing the same things'. However, one student is reading *imaginatively*, analysing *thoughtfully*, and writing *carefully*; whilst the other student is reading *unimaginatively*, analysing *thoughtlessly*, and writing *carelessly*. The former student is on the way to developing the virtues of inquiry; the latter student is on the way to developing the vices of inquiry. In other words, the quality of attention given to one's practice relates directly to how one's agency is related to it—whether the present activity is seen by the agent as merely a burdensome means to a future end, or as something that is loved for its own sake.

In particular, as Holt discusses in detail in *How Children Fail*, if *fear* is a dominant external motive for children in schooling—as it too often is—then that is enormously destructive of their intelligence. In Holt's words, "the scared learner is always a poor learner" (Holt 1982, p. 93). Consider his comments about 'Emily':

> The child *must* be right. She cannot bear to be wrong, or even to imagine that she might be wrong. ... When she is told to do something, she does it quickly and fearfully, hands it to some higher authority, and awaits the magic word *right* or *wrong*. If the word is *right*, she does not have to think about that problem anymore; if the word is *wrong*, she does not want to, cannot bring herself to think about it. (Holt 1982, pp. 21–2)

As Holt remarks, if an agent is motivated by fear (of getting a wrong answer) this is productive of various vices of inquiry: it tends to produce an agent who, like Emily, is defensive, evasive, helpless, and passive. In Holt's words,

> The strategies of most of these kids have been consistently self-centred, self-protective, aimed above all else at avoiding trouble, embarrassment, punishment, disapproval, or loss of status. (Holt 1982, p. 91)

And, as he importantly notes, "Strategy is an outgrowth of character" (Holt 1982, p. 87). That is, in the terms I have used here, *how* an agent approaches an inquiry is a function of the virtues and vices of inquiry that she possesses. Is the agent intellectually courageous, patient, tenacious, and resourceful? Or, like many of the children that Holt wrote about, is the agent timid, inflexible, and passive?

Holt's argument that the instrumentalism of education systematically provides incentives for developing the vices of inquiry can be seen—as Holt himself notes—as a radicalisation of Dewey's principle of the 'continuity of experience'. Although, as remarked in the previous chapter, I have no intention of attempting to set Holt systematically in the context of other child-centred or 'progressive' forms of educational philosophy, this particular relationship to Deweyan thought is worth briefly commenting on here. Most comprehensively in *Experience and Education*, Dewey argued that the kinds of experience through which learning occurred were crucial, because they played a role in the formation of the *person* of the learner. As Dewey writes,

> At bottom, this principle rests upon the fact of habit, when *habit* is interpreted biologically. The basic characteristic of habit is that every experience enacted and undergone modifies the one who acts and undergoes, while this modification affects, whether we wish it or not, the quality of subsequent experiences. For it is a somewhat different person who enters into them. The principle of habit so understood obviously goes deeper than the ordinary conception of *a* habit as a more or less fixed way of doing things, although it includes the latter as one of its special cases. It covers the formation of attitudes, attitudes that are emotional and intellectual; it covers our basic sensitivities and ways of meeting and responding to all the conditions which we meet in living. (Dewey 2015, p. 35)

"Hence", writes Dewey, "the central problem of an education based upon experience is to select the kind of present experiences that live fruitfully and creatively in subsequent experiences" (2015, pp. 27–8). Dewey thus shares with Holt, then, the thought that the relationship between education and the learner's character is of particular importance. However, as Dewey's language of 'habit' and 'modification' in the passage just quoted indicate, he conceives of the learner as essentially passive. The learner is, for Dewey, the *subject* of experiences, who is causally modified by them. The active person in Dewey's model is thus the educator, who designs an educational context in order to 'select' the right (growth-oriented) experiences that will then 'form' the learner's attitudes. In contrast, as argued in this chapter, Holt has a much richer account of the relations between activity and character—and, in particular, how character relates to the learner's agency. Hence, the crucial difference between Dewey and Holt is that, for Holt, the learner is not a subject but the *actor*; rather than being transformed by experiences, the learner transforms *herself* through her own activity (in engaging passionately with various human practices and pursuing their internal goods).

Closer to Holt's perspective is the thought of another Deweyan, the influential William Kilpatrick. In his famous paper 'The project method' (1918), Kilpatrick argues that the best form of learning comes from "wholehearted purposeful activity proceeding in a social environment, or more briefly, in the unit element of such activity, the hearty purposeful act" (Kilpatrick 1918, p. 320). Hence, he argues,

> If the purposeful act be in reality the typical unit of the worthy life, then it follows that to base education on purposeful acts is exactly to identify the process of education with worthy living itself. The two become then the same. (Kilpatrick 1918, p. 323)

That is, as Holt would agree, 'living is learning'. Kilpatrick thus shares with Holt the emphasis on the importance of the learner's exercise of agency—of engaging in activity in a way that is "wholehearted" and driven by "the presence of a dominating purpose" (Kilpatrick 1918, p. 321)—and how the quality of engagement plays a role in shaping the learner's character. However, Kilpatrick's account of the relationships between agency, activity, and character are conceptually crude. Under the influence of a mechanistic psychology that only here and there resembles a human being, he views 'wholeheartedness' as a simple ordinal variable, and claims that the "psychological value [of a learner's activity] increases with the degree of approximation to 'wholeheartedness'" (Kilpatrick 1918, p. 322). Entirely missing from Kilpatrick's account are the distinctions—so crucial to understanding Holt's position—between instrumental and autotelic activity, external and internal goods. After all, a learner could engage in an activity in 'wholehearted' pursuit of an instrumental good, such as gaining high grades. But this is not a situation that will encourage that learner to develop the virtues of a practice. In fact, it will tend to encourage the development of the various and all-too-familiar vices of the over-schooled: slavish rule-following, unimaginativeness, dependence on the expectations of authorities, lack of originality, fear of genuinely critical thought, and the like.

2.10 Conclusion

The argument of this chapter has been long and complex, so a summary may be found useful. In this chapter I have constructed an Aristotelian model of agency and activity in order to make clear and coherent sense of Holt's account of learning and his critique of education. The main results of the analysis are as follows:

1. Holt holds that there is a kind of learning that is particularly valuable and important. This learning is the agent's development of her character, through acquiring the *virtues* of practices.
2. This 'best learning' can only be acquired by undertaking those practices in pursuit of their internal goods. It cannot be acquired through instrumental activity (that is, by undertaking a practice as an efficient means to some external good).
3. That is, this 'best learning' is essentially a by-product of activities pursued for themselves, or autotelically—that is, because the agent loves the activity for itself, and thus engages in it passionately or wholeheartedly.
4. Hence, external incentives and disincentives (grades, threats of punishment, etc.)—such as are typical of educational practice—cannot produce the 'best learning'. Insofar as students manage to acquire the 'best learning' in an (instrumentalised) educational context, they do so in spite of that context rather than because of it.
5. Furthermore, engaging in practices out of such instrumental motives tends to encourage the agent to develop the vices of the practice in question.
6. In the case of practices of inquiry, possessing the vices of that practice (to a significant degree) is (a form of) stupidity.
7. Hence, educational practice, insofar as it relies on instrumental motives, tends to 'make students stupid'.

This account of Holt's position still remains, however, rather abstract. To make it somewhat more concrete is the job of the rest of this book. The next chapter (Chap. 3) will fill in further details of Holt's account, by way of responses to the most salient and significant objections to that account. The final chapter (Chap. 4) will then briefly examine the practical strategies—homeschooling, in particular—that Holt recommends for mitigating the problems with education that are diagnosed by his account, and for improving children's chances of acquiring 'the best learning'.

References

Aristotle (1984). *Nichomachean ethics* (W. D. Ross, Trans.). In J Barnes (Ed.), *The complete works of Aristotle: The revised Oxford translation*. Princeton, NJ: Princeton University Press.
Baehr, J. (2011). *The inquiring mind: On intellectual virtues and virtue epistemology*. Oxford: Oxford University Press.
Barrow, R. (1978). *Radical education: A critique of freeschooling and deschooling*. Oxford: Martin Robertson.
Brewer, T. (2009). *The retrieval of ethics*. Oxford: Oxford University Press.
Burnyeat, M. F. (1980). Aristotle on learning to be good. In A. O. Rorty (Ed.), *Essays on Aristotle's Ethics* (pp. 69–92). Berkeley, CA: University of California Press.
Crawford, M. (2010). *Shopcraft as soulcraft: An inquiry into the value of work*. London: Penguin.
Dewey, J. (2015). *Experience and education*. New York: Simon and Schuster.
Elster, J. (1983). *Sour grapes: Studies in the subversion of rationality*. Cambridge: Cambridge University Press.
Foot, P. (2002). Virtues and vices. *Virtues and vices and other essays in moral philosophy* (pp. 1–18). Oxford: Clarendon Press.
Green, B. (1986). *The inner game of music*. New York: Doubleday.
Hirst, P. (1975). What is teaching? In R. S. Peters (Ed.), *The philosophy of education* (pp. 163–77). London: Routledge and Kegan Paul.
Holt, J. (1970). *What do I do Monday?* New York: E. P. Dutton and Co.
Holt, J. (1971). Big bird, meet Dick and Jane: A critique of Sesame Street. *Atlantic Monthly, 227*(5), 72–8.
Holt, J. (1972). Fundamental reminders: We learn for ourselves. *Edcentric: A Journal for Educational Change, September*, 4–6.
Holt, J. (1976). *Instead of education*. New York: E. P. Dutton and Co.
Holt, J. (1981). *Teach your own: A hopeful path for education*. Liss, Hants: Lighthouse Books.
Holt, J. (1982). *How children fail* (revised ed.). New York: Merloyd Lawrence.
Holt, J. (1983). *How children learn* (revised ed.). London: Penguin.
Holt, J. (1989). *Learning all the time*. New York: Merloyd Lawrence.
Holt, J. (1990). Letter to Joanna Picciotto, 1/1/82. In S. Sheffer (Ed.), *A life worth living: Selected letters of John Holt* (pp. 249–52). Columbus, OH: Ohio State University Press.
Hookway, C. (2003). How to be a virtue epistemologist. In M. DePaul & L. Zagzebski (Eds.), *Intellectual virtue: Perspectives from ethics and epistemology* (pp. 183–202). Oxford: Oxford University Press.
Kilpatrick, W. H. (1918). The project method. *Teachers College Record, 19*(4), 319–35.
MacIntyre, A. (1984). *After virtue: A study in moral theory* (2nd ed.). Notre Dame, IN: University of Notre Dame Press.
MacIntyre, A. (1994). The *Theses on Feuerbach*: A road not taken. In C. C. Gould & R. S. Cohen (Eds.), *Artifacts, representations and social practice* (pp. 277–90). Dordrecht: Kluwer.
Marsalis, W. (1995). *Marsalis on music*. New York: Norton.
Peters, R. S. (1966). *Ethics and education*. London: George Allen and Unwin.
Pirsig, R. M. (2004). *Zen and the art of motorcycle maintenance: An inquiry into values* (25th anniversary ed.). London: Vintage.
Roberts, R. C., & Wood, W. J. (2007). *Intellectual virtues: An essay in regulative epistemology*. Oxford: Oxford University Press.
Sennett, R. (2008). *The craftsman*. New Haven, CT: Yale University Press.
Sudnow, D. (2001). *Ways of the hand: A rewritten account*. Cambridge, MA: MIT Press.
Von Wright, G. H. (1963). *The varieties of goodness*. London: Routledge and Kegan Paul.
Wittgenstein, L. (1958). *Philosophische Untersuchungen/Philosophical Investigations* (2nd ed.). (G. E. M. Anscombe, Trans.). Oxford: Basil Blackwell.
Wood, L. (1963). Intelligence. In D. D. Runes (Ed.), *Dictionary of philosophy*. New York: Philosophical Library.

Chapter 3
Objections and Replies

> … the small child's sense of the wholeness and openness of life is … his most human trait. It is above all else what makes it possible for him—or anyone else—to grow and learn. (Holt 1970, p. 24)

3.1 Introduction

In this chapter I consider a number of potential objections to Holt's views on learning and education. In a change of mode, the chapter is not a continuous exposition. Instead, I first state an objection and then give a relatively self-contained essay in answer to it. The aim of these essays is not simply the negative work of rebuttal and refutation. Rather, through answering each objection, the chapter as a whole aims to enrich and extend the abstract framework provided in the previous chapter. In other words, this is a continuation of the previous chapter's exposition of Holt's views, but done in a somewhat more dialogical manner.

3.2 Objection #1: Childish desires

According to this account, for the 'best learning' to be acquired, learners need to engage in a practice for its own sake—in pursuit of the internal goods of that practice. But that is a very sophisticated, adult desire to have—and children, after all, have childish desires. Hence, whilst engaging in practices for their own sake may be an appropriate aim for adult learners, it is not so for young children.

There are two connected errors that lie behind this objection. First, it mistakes the sophistication of the analytical framework—or, rather, the language in which that framework is expressed—for the sophistication of the phenomena being described. Stated more plainly, all this talk in the previous chapter of 'agency', 'internal goods' versus 'external motivations', 'practices', and 'autotelic activity' may not be ordinary and everyday; but it is part of a philosophical analysis of something that *is* ordinary and everyday. The second error lying behind the objection is that it misses the significance of the fact that human practices are *dialectical* in nature—that through engaging in a practice, one's grasp of its internal standards of excellence grows in depth and sophistication.

The first point is easily dealt with. Whilst the Aristotelian language in which this point is expressed may not be familiar to all, to engage in a practice 'in pursuit of its internal goods', 'in pursuit of its internal standards of excellence', or 'for its own sake' is an everyday phenomenon. Some examples should help to make this clear:

> If one is reading a novel that one loves, then the aim of the activity is the reading itself—to read with as much attention and care as possible, immersing oneself in the language and the story. It is not, for example, simply 'to find out what happens'—for in that case, it would be far more efficient to read a plot summary, or skip to the last chapter.

> If one is building a piece of fine wooden furniture as a gift for a loved one then the aim is to bring the project to completion; but it is to do this by building it as carefully and skilfully as one can (attempting to do full justice to the beauty of the grain; by being as precise as one can with the joinery, etc.). The fact that the agent, in this imagined case, would reject as offensive the idea of simply *purchasing* a piece of furniture (even if that were more 'efficient') shows that this activity is being pursued autotelically, not instrumentally.

> For someone who loves cooking, then the aim of that activity is indeed that a meal be prepared—but it is to be prepared by way of the activity of the agent himself cooking as well as he possibly can (taking pains to bring out the best in the ingredients; cooking the meat just so; balancing the flavours, etc.). In this imagined case, the cooking is not undertaken simply as an efficient means to the end of 'having a meal prepared'—and this is shown in the fact that the agent would scornfully reject the suggestion that 'it would be more efficient' simply to purchase some takeaway food or hire in a cook for the day.

> If one is playing a piece of music, then the aim is to play that music as well as possible—playing it with the right sort of expressiveness, tone, rhythm, etc. The playing of the music is not simply an efficient means to the end of 'having music played'—for in that case, simply hitting a button on a stereo would achieve the end far more efficiently than all the work of practice, tuning, maintaining the instrument, etc.

> When one plays a game such as chess, then the aim is to win (of course), but it is to win by playing the best chess one can play (rather than, for example, by cheating, or by paying one's opponent to deliberately lose—even if this could be shown to be a 'more efficient' path to a win).

In each of these cases, the central point of doing the activity is to do it as well as one can; in Aristotelian terms, in each case, the agent is aiming at *excellence* in that activity. In each case, the measure of what counts as 'doing the activity well' or 'excellence', comes from within the practice itself—what counts as excellent reading, cooking, woodwork, music-making, and so on. That is to say, in each case one is aiming at the *internal goods* of the activity. This is so, even when the activity also produces an outcome (such as a win, or a piece of fine furniture, or a delicious meal, or a good musical performance). This is because the outcome *in itself* was not the motive—as we only desired the outcome *through undertaking the activity* (rather than achieving it in some other way, such as by purchasing it as a commodity). That is, the activity is engaged in autotelically, rather than instrumentally (as an efficient means to an end). It is a revealing fact that, in many of these imagined cases, attempting to treat them as if they were purely instrumental (by suggesting 'more efficient means') is not simply a missing of the point—it is a missing of the point that can be deeply *ethically* offensive, for it demonstrates a failure to understand how the activity fits into a good human life.

It is worth emphasising that the assumption made in each of the above examples is that the agent is engaged in the activities in a particular way—namely, with care, attention, seriousness, focus, or love; rather than idly, frivolously, inattentively, half-heartedly, or distractedly. This is because to engage in a practice 'seriously', 'with care, focus, attention', or, most strongly, 'with love for what one is doing' are simply alternative names for what has been termed here 'engaging in a practice in pursuit of its internal goods'. Words like 'care', 'focus' and 'love' (and so on) refer to the agent's on-going attentiveness and responsiveness to those internal goods. For to talk of 'internal goods' is to talk about those things that make the practice worth doing (for that agent)—they are what the agent cares about; what she is attending to; what she values; what she loves.

Let us now return to the objection that children have 'childish' desires, and therefore lack the sophistication to desire such internal goods. As mentioned above, what this misses is the point that human practices are dialectical. What this means, to recall the previous chapter's discussions, is that the internal goods of a practice are (if all goes well) *progressively* revealed to the agent, by her on-going engagement in the practice. So, for example, I come to grasp the internal goods of music-making—or, what excellence in music-making demands of me—through making music. That is, agents begin a practice with only the most inchoate, inarticulate sense of its internal goods, but then that sense develops, ramifies, becomes more sophisticated, through the agent's engagement in the practice.

This point about the dialectical nature of practices, helps us to see the kind of unities, or continuities, that exist in human activity. The most sophisticated forms of human practices have their origins in fundamental human desires and motivations; those practices are immensely complex developments, or elaborations, of much simpler or more basic activities and desires. As Holt repeatedly emphasises, the most sophisticated sorts of inquiry—in physics and chemistry, for example—have their roots in fundamental human feelings of wonder and curiosity, and are developments of the most basic forms of inquiry that humans engage in. Holt thus writes that,

> children have a passionate desire to understand as much of the world as they can, even what they cannot see and touch, and as far as possible to acquire some kind of skill, competence, and control in it and over it. (Holt 1989, p. 159)

And that,

> Children are born passionately eager to make as much sense as they can of things around them. The process by which children turn experience into knowledge is exactly the same, point for point, as the process by which those whom we call scientists make scientific knowledge. Children observe, they wonder, they speculate, and they ask themselves questions. They think up possible answers, they make theories, they hypothesise, and then they test theories by asking questions or by further observations or experiments or reading. Then they modify the theories as needed, or reject them, and the process continues. (Holt 1989, p. 94)

And, a final example of this theme in Holt's work, that,

telling the child he had to study Physics in order to find out about the jet engine would be like telling him he had to study initial and final consonants, digraphs, and blends in order to find out what words say and mean. With such advice we cut him off from his intention, his purpose, send him on a long detour. We put things backwards. Physics is not going to lead the child to jet engines, but wondering about jet planes will lead him to Physics. In fact, wondering about jet planes *is* Physics. The child asking such a question *is doing Physics*. (Holt 1976, p. 84)

The child's passionate desires to understand, to make sense of things—the sense of curiosity and wonder at the world—are the starting point for all forms of human inquiry. That is, the point that Holt is making in these quoted passages is not that children are highly sophisticated scientists, but that our highly sophisticated sciences (and all the other varied disciplines of inquiry that we have made) are developments (immensely complex ones) of fundamental forms of human motivation. Our most complex forms of inquiry are thus, in crucially important ways, *continuous* with the most basic ways in which even the very youngest of human beings attempt to make sense of the world around them. They are, that is, a dialectical development of the same practice—a dialectical elaboration of the child's wonder and curiosity. Hence, as Holt writes, "'Science', of course, is not the private property of 'scientists', but something that we all do when we are trying to solve some kind of problem or puzzle" (Holt 1989, p. 134). Approaching this same point from the other direction, the great physicist Ernst Mach writes, "Where does heat come from? Where does heat go to? The questions of children [*Kinderfragen*] in the mouths of mature adults shape the character of a century" (Mach, 1903, p. 229; my translation).

This dialectical development can be seen in the history of our practices of inquiry. For example, the questions of the pre-Socratics—such as, *What is the world made of? Where did the world come from?*—are, on the one hand, the beginnings of science, and, on the other hand, recognisably childlike. Or consider, for example, Gareth Matthews's work on doing philosophy with children (Matthews 1992), which shows that very young children, without elaborate prompting, quite naturally engage in philosophical talk and reasoning. That is, "not proto-philosophical, or quasi-philosophical, or semi-philosophical, it is the real thing" (Matthews 1994, p. 34). This would not have surprised Plato's Socrates in the least, for he knew well that "wonder is where philosophy begins and nowhere else" (Plato 1961, 155c).

These considerations can be extended to all human practices—music, for example. Of course children do not begin with the sophisticated desires of an experienced musician (e.g., a desire to syncopate a particular passage in the right way). But they do begin with something that we might express as being a desire *to make a glorious noise*—as, for example, is clearly recognised in Carl Orff's influential works on "Musik für Kinder" (e.g., Orff and Keetman 1950). The complex desires of the mature musician are recognisably descended from childlike motivations like this. The practice of music making, in other words, in all its great complexity and richness, can be seen as a dialectical development of motivations possessed by very young children, and their basic responses to such things as melody and rhythm.

Hence, the answer to the objection under consideration is as follows. It is, of course, true that children do not possess the complex, sophisticated desires of experienced adult practitioners of a practice. But the highly complex activities in which these practitioners engage are recognisably descended from much more basic forms of the very same practice. It is through engaging in those practices in their most basic, fundamental forms—in engaging in basic forms of inquiry, for example—that those childlike forms of the desires (of wonder and curiosity, for example) will begin to ramify, deepen, and become more articulate. Eventually (if all goes well) they will become the complex motivations of a mature practitioner. In sum, contrary to the claim made in the objection, young children *do* possess desires for the internal goods of human practices, but they possess these desires in inchoate forms. The dialectical nature of our practices means that the motivations of the young child and those of the sophisticated practitioner exist on a continuum, rather than being separated by a gulf. Or, to put this another way, the central desires of children are not in the least *childish*, but profoundly *human*. In Holt's words,

> Unless warped by cruelty or neglect, children are *by nature* ... serious and purposeful. ... Just about everything [very little children] do, they do as well as they can. Except when tired or hungry, or in the grip of passion, pain, or fear, they are moved to act almost entirely by curiosity, desire for mastery and competence, and pride in work well done. But the schools, and many adults outside of school, hardly ever recognise or honour such motives, can hardly even imagine that they exist. In their place they put Greed and Fear. (Holt 1981, p. 113)

Hence Holt's confidence that, given the right surroundings, children will "find *within themselves* their reasons for doing worthwhile things" (Holt 1981, p. 113).

As a way of drawing this essay to a close, it is worth remarking here how Holt's view of the profound continuity that exists between children's practices of inquiry, and those of sophisticated practitioners, sidesteps a significant problem that exists for those liberal philosophies of education that focus on the achievement of *autonomy* as the primary goal of education. These views descend from Kant, who draws a sharp distinction between 'heteronomy' and 'autonomy'. For Kant, heteronomy was a state of being ruled by one's desires (thus seen as 'external' to one's self), whilst autonomy was a state of being ruled by *reason*—which, for Kant, was genuine human freedom and agency. This dichotomy thus entails that, for a Kantian, education is a site of profound tension—because it is supposed to lead children from one side of this dichotomy to the other. Children begin, in this picture, as existing in a state of heteronomy, driven by their desires. They therefore need to be disciplined and controlled through external motivations ('bribe' and 'threat', in other words), as appeals to reason are ineffective. However, the whole *raison d'être* of this constraint is, somehow, to transform them into autonomous adults. Hence, for a Kantian, education must answer the question: "How do I cultivate freedom under constraint?" (Kant 2007, 9: 453). And in case it is thought that this picture is a relic of the eighteenth century, it is worth pointing out that we find precisely the same dichotomy at work, for example, in Amy Gutmann's influential book *Democratic Education*. She writes there that, "The earliest education of children is not and cannot be by precept or reasoning; it must be by discipline and example" (Gutmann 1999, p. 50); hence, "Being educated as a child entails being ruled" (p. 3).

It should be clear by now that Holt rejects this Kantian picture root and branch. For reasons we have explored in the previous chapter, he argues that the external imposition of constraint and discipline in learning does not help to produce 'autonomous adults'. Rather, such imposition is a breeding ground for vices of inquiry such as passivity, helplessness, inflexibility, and intellectual cowardice. Furthermore, his view entails that there is no dichotomous split between 'desire' and 'reason', and hence no need to seek for some bridge to lead children from one side to the other. Rather, children possess certain strong desires—wonder and curiosity, in particular—which, in the right circumstances, are a direct road to those practices and intellectual virtues that deserve the title of rationality. Hence the invalidity of Guttmann's reasoning in the passage quoted above. She is right that the earliest education of children cannot be 'by precept or reasoning', but that does not entail that it *must* be 'by discipline and example'. For, given the right surroundings, children can follow (some of) their desires, without external compulsion—do what strikes them as significant, valuable and worth doing—and yet learn what they need to learn.

3.3 Objection #2: Disagreeable Hard Work

Learning a practice always involves—especially at the start—disagreeable hard work, and children have not yet learned the capacity for deferred gratification. Hence, they need external motivation for learning; intrinsic motivation comes later, with growing maturity and acquired steadiness of purpose.

This is a very important objection to discuss, because it embodies a conception of pleasure and its relation to activity that is both deeply instrumentalist, and profoundly influential. An analysis of Holt's attack on this conception will provide further details of the Aristotelian nature of his views about agency, and its relation to love for what one does.

The key assumptions at work in this objection can be schematically presented by way of the following diagram (which I adapt from Elster 1986, p. 105):

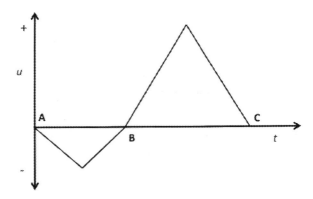

In this graph, the horizontal axis (labelled 't') is *time*. The vertical axis (labelled 'u') is *utility*, which is economists' jargon for what, in more ordinary language, might

3.3 Objection #2: Disagreeable Hard Work

be called 'pleasure' or 'satisfaction'. Above the junction with the horizontal axis is 'positive utility'; below is 'negative utility' (i.e., displeasure, or dissatisfaction). The progression of time—from A, to B, to C—represents (in a very simplified, schematic form) an agent's engagement in a practice. At the beginning (the interval A–B), the agent is learning basic skills and the work is hard and unpleasant; the agent obtains only negative utility from the activity. But at a certain point (B), this investment of effort begins to pay off, and, thanks to her greater skills, the agent begins to obtain pleasure from the activity. Eventually, 'hedonic adaptation' sets in and the practice becomes boring or pleasureless to the agent (C).[1] Taken as a whole (the interval A–C), the learning of the practice has been worth doing, because the total amount of pleasure (represented here as the area between the horizontal axis and the line from B to C) that the agent obtains, is greater than her total amount of displeasure (represented here as the area between the horizontal axis and the line from A to B).

To make this schema less abstract, let us consider an example; say, learning to play the cello. The thought is then that, at the beginning, the cello playing is only a source of dissatisfaction or displeasure to the agent—it is, that is to say, disagreeable hard work. She struggles to hit the notes with accuracy, has to take great efforts even to play short passages of simple music, her hands and forearms quickly get sore; in sum, she is unable to play in any way that gives her pleasure. However, if she perseveres with this frustration, she will reach a point (B) where she will start to get pleasure from her music-making—her fingers can find the right notes with ease; she can play more complex and therefore interesting pieces; she no longer finds the music-making as physically and mentally taxing.

Now, given this model, we can make clear sense of what the objection is claiming. It is saying that children (typically? always?) are not prepared, off their own bats, to make the investment of time and effort represented by the interval A–B. That is, they are not prepared to commit to the investment of this disagreeable hard work, even though, if they were to do this, there would be a pay-off of lots of pleasure or satisfaction for them forthcoming in interval B–C. To be incapable of putting up with displeasure in the short term, so as to be able to gain greater pleasure in the long term, is to lack the capacity for deferred gratification. The lack of this capacity is, as Frank Ramsey puts it in a classic discussion, a "weakness of the imagination" (Ramsey 1928, p. 543): one is so consumed by the present displeasure (in A–B) that one is unable to make 'living' (and hence motivating) for oneself the thought of the much greater pleasure to come (in B–C).

Given the supposed lack of this capacity in children, it would therefore seem to be an appropriate role for educators to incentivise children so that they will do the disagreeable hard work required to start gaining utility from the practice. That is, the educator's role would be to provide external motivations so that children will get to B, at which point internal motivations (i.e., the utility obtained by the agent from the activity) can take over. The educator can thus say, with truth, "I am doing this for your own good, and you will thank me for it in the future".

---

[1] Elster's assumption of hedonic adaptation is not essential to the point being made; the agent's pleasure could flatten out, rather than declining back to zero.

According to the objection, then, Holt's whole model of the 'best learning' and critique of education make sense only on the assumption that children have the capacity for deferred gratification, but this is not something they tend to possess. Therefore much important learning (especially at the early stages) needs to proceed via the impetus provided by external motivations. And therefore children need professional teachers, compulsory schooling, the Department of Education, and the rest …

Holt's response to this objection is to point out that the very idea of 'deferred gratification' takes for granted the instrumentalist conception of activity that he rejects. This is because it conceptualises pleasure (utility, satisfaction) as an *external* good and the activity as a *means* to that external good. That is, it treats the pleasure as something that is conceptually separable from the activity, and 'produced' by the activity as a 'goal' or 'output'. The pleasure thereby provides the motive or incentive for the agent to undertake the activity (or provides a disincentive, in the case of displeasure). In doing this, the objection treats effort as something that an agent finds unpleasant, and hence will engage in only in return for an adequate 'pay off'. Holt thinks this entire model—with its instrumentalist conception of the relation between activity, effort, and pleasure—is utterly mistaken. As he writes,

> They say that to do anything takes Disagreeable Hard Work, that all work is Disagreeable Hard Work. In those three words is a whole way of life and of looking at life, very widespread, very deeply rooted, and very wrong. (Holt 1972, p. 110)

The way to dig out this deeply rooted instrumentalism is to begin with a reconceptualisation of the notion of pleasure. Once again, Aristotle offers us the best starting point for this. In the *Nichomachean Ethics*, he argues that the pleasure we take in activity is not a separate 'sensation', which is *produced* by our doings. Rather, Aristotle writes, "pleasure *completes* the activity" (Aristotle 1984, 1175a5; my emphasis), and that it "supervenes" on the activity "as the bloom of youth does on those in the flower of their age" (1174b33). For this reason, pleasure in an activity is conceptually tied to the *love* of an activity—in that "each kind of person finds pleasure in whatever he is called a lover of" (1099a8-9).

Gilbert Ryle gives a clear account of what Aristotle means by this talk of pleasure as 'completing' and 'supervening' on an activity. In *The Concept of Mind*, and in his 1954 paper "Pleasure", Ryle argues that to take pleasure in an activity, or to enjoy it, is not for certain sensations to accompany the activity, or result from it. Rather, it is to *perform the activity in a certain way*, namely, to perform it wholeheartedly, or in a deeply absorbed way. He writes that,

> when a child is absorbed in a game he—every drop of him—is sucked up into the business of manipulating his clockwork trains. … His game is, for the moment, his whole world. (Ryle 2009, p. 346)

And this absorption just *is* for that child to enjoy, or take pleasure in, that game. For,

> to say that a person has been enjoying digging is not to say that he has been both digging and doing or experiencing something else as a concomitant or effect of the digging; it is to say that he dug with his whole heart in his task, i.e. that he dug, wanting to dig and not wanting to do anything else. (Ryle 1990, p. 104)

3.3 Objection #2: Disagreeable Hard Work

Hence, Ryle concludes,

> we say that a person who is so absorbed in some activity, such as golf or argument, that he is reluctant to stop, or even to think of anything else, is 'taking pleasure in' or 'enjoying' what he is doing. (Ryle 1990, p. 104)

As Talbot Brewer points out, Ryle's verbal formulation here is potentially misleading. Imagine a person performing an activity under threat of death. No doubt this person would be reluctant to stop, and would indeed be likely to be absorbed in that activity. However, we would hardly talk of a person in such circumstances 'taking pleasure' in the activity. Brewer thus suggests that a better way of capturing Ryle's point is to say that,

> to take pleasure in an activity is to engage in that activity while being absorbed in it, where this absorption consists in single-minded and lively attention to whatever it is that makes the activity good or worth pursuing. (Brewer 2009, p. 116)

This formulation captures not just the sense in which 'taking pleasure in' a certain activity 'completes' or 'supervenes on' the activity, but also Aristotle's point about the connection between taking pleasure in an activity and the agent's love of that activity. Taking pleasure in an activity is to be deeply absorbed in that activity for its own sake (i.e., for the sake of the internal goods of that activity); that is, it is for an agent to do it wholeheartedly, out of love for the activity. Pleasure thus lies in the *quality of attention* that an agent brings to an activity.

There are closely related thoughts in another of the great critics of instrumentalism, Karl Marx. In the *Grundrisse*, Marx discusses Adam Smith's assumption that human beings naturally prefer 'ease' or 'leisure', and therefore require incentives in order to engage in anything requiring effort. In capitalism, of course, this incentive is a wage. This thought of Smith's directly parallels the model of deferred gratification discussed above, except in this latter case, the incentive or 'wage' is the promised future pay-off of pleasure or utility. For Marx, the instrumentalist split between 'leisure' and 'work'—which is given social reality in a capitalist economy—is simultaneously a degradation of both human activity, and pleasure. This is because, on the one hand, it reduces pleasure to "mere fun"—an end to be derived from trivial "amusement"; whilst making genuinely effortful activity a mere means for earning a wage, undertaken only under compulsion. In contrast, Marx writes, "Really free working, e.g., composing, is at the same time the most damned serious, intensive exertion", for the "overcoming of obstacles is in itself a liberating activity" (Marx 1973, p. 611). That is, given the right social circumstances, humans will *freely choose* to engage in activities that require great effort, and will take great joy in that doing. With these words of Marx in mind, consider the following passage from Holt about his great love, music:

> The assumption is that while playing music we vary from the 'no fun' end of the scale to the 'fun' end. If we spend 99 percent of our time at the 'no fun' end of the scale, eventually we will get to the point where we have a little fun. I think this is a disastrously mistaken way of looking at music. Nowhere on that scale of 'no fun' to 'fun' can I find any of the emotions that I feel when I am working with my cello. These range from arduous effort to intense concentration, great frustration and exasperation to something that can only be called

exaltation. There are feelings so deep that one can barely play the music. You can't use the word *fun* to describe that range of feeling. (Holt 1989, pp. 123–4)

What these thinkers—Aristotle, Marx, Ryle, Brewer—show us, is that the claim that children cannot engage in practices because they 'lack a capacity for deferred gratification' is itself a result of a weakness of the imagination. This is because such a claim can only conceive of agency and motivation in instrumental terms, viewing the agent's activity as a means for maximising pleasure (or utility). However, what Aristotle and the others remind us, is that we are not forced to think of matters in this way. Instead, we can recapture the thought that—in the magnificent words of Albert Borgmann (1984, p. 202)—when engaging wholeheartedly in human practices, the agent finds that her "effort and joy are one; the split between means and ends, labor and leisure is healed".

Holt is part of this alternative tradition of non-instrumental ways of thinking of activity and agency, and the thoughts sketched above can help us to see the clear sense in what he says about 'deferred gratification'. To begin with, Holt points to the obvious empirical fact that children just *do* engage in activities that demand great effort. Indeed, as he reminds us, it is one of the salient characteristics of young children that they live with great intensity, throwing the whole of themselves into what they do. It is thus common to find them "in that dreamlike state children get into when they are really absorbed in something. [In which] Time meant nothing" (Holt 1983, p. 265). Hence, as Holt writes,

> Anyone who has known many children growing up knows that many of them, even though they may not have much time of their own after school and schoolwork, throw themselves with great energy and discipline into very demanding kinds of work, often much harder than the work they can't or don't do in school, often involving the very 'skills' that the school says they don't have and can't learn. (Holt 1972, p. 115)

Or, in another passage from the same book,

> We hear constantly that children will never do anything unless compelled to by bribes or threats. But in their private lives, or in extracurricular activities in school, in sports, music, drama, art, running a newspaper, and so on, they often submit themselves willingly and wholeheartedly to very intense disciplines. (Holt 1972, p. 109)

Holt also argues against the idea—embedded in the model of delayed gratification discussed above—that the initial stages of a difficult venture *must* involve unpleasantness, some sense of "uphill struggle" or "going against the grain", and that "satisfaction" comes later (as claimed in Elster 1985, p. 89). Holt suggests that it is only when instrumentalist conceptions of 'success' and 'failure' raise their head, that this is the case. For example, he writes that,

> Babies learning to walk, and falling down as they try, or healthy six- and seven-year-olds learning to ride a bike, and falling off, do not think, each time they fall, "I failed again". Healthy babies or children, tackling difficult projects of their own choosing, think only when they fall down or off, "Oops, not yet, try again". Nor do they think, when finally they begin to walk or ride, "Oh, boy, I'm succeeding!" They think, "Now I'm walking! Now I'm riding!" *The joy is in the act itself*, the walking or the riding, not in some idea of success. ... Children ... do not think in terms of success and failure but of effort and adventure. (Holt 1982, pp. 69–70; my emphasis)

3.3 Objection #2: Disagreeable Hard Work

Or, consider this passage from *Escape From Childhood*, with its echoes of the statements from Marx and Borgmann quoted above:

> there is something very appealing and exciting about watching children just learning to walk. They do it so badly, it is so clearly difficult, and in the child's terms may even be dangerous. ... Most adults, even many older children, would instantly stop trying to do anything that they did as badly as a new walker does his walking. But the infant keeps on. He is so determined, he is working so hard, and he is so excited; his learning to walk is *not just an effort and struggle but a joyous adventure*. (Holt 1974, pp. 119–20; my emphasis)

These obvious empirical facts only appear difficult to explain if one is wedded to the instrumentalist conceptions of activity and pleasure. We do not need to ascribe to these children some complex feat of rationality and imagination, in which they are calculating the total amount of future pleasure to be gained from walking or riding and weighing that against the current displeasure of investing an effort in learning to do this. Rather than this preposterous picture of the child as a miniature *Homo economicus*, we simply need to remind ourselves that these children are doing things they want to do—often things that are "the most damned serious, intensive exertion"—and doing them wholeheartedly—and that this just *is* what it is to take pleasure in what one is doing. That is, to repeat Borgmann's words, in such activities the children's effort and their joy are one and the same. Hence, as Holt concludes,

> It is a serious mistake to say that, in order to learn, children must first be able to 'delay gratification' ... It is their desire and determination to do real things, not in the future but right now, that gives children the curiosity, energy, determination, and patience to learn all they learn. (Holt 1983, p. 288)

Applied to children's learning, the instrumentalist model of 'disagreeable hard work' and 'delayed gratification' produces a degraded conception of human motivation, and this, in turn, encourages the learner to develop a degraded conception of her own agency. Holt writes of this that,

> The idea that children won't learn without outside rewards and penalties, or in the debased jargon of the behaviourists, 'positive and negative reinforcements', usually becomes a self-fulfilling prophecy. If we treat children long enough *as if* that were true, they will come to believe it is true. So many people have said to me, "If we didn't make children do things, they wouldn't do anything". Even worse, they say, "If *I* weren't made to do things, *I* wouldn't do anything". *It is the creed of a slave*. (Holt 1982, p. 113)

As we have seen, an instrumentalist conception involves a view of the agent as motivated only by external goods (such as money, status, pleasure) and engaging in activities because they appear as efficient means for achieving these goods. From an Aristotelian standpoint this is, quite literally, to conceive of one's own activity *slavishly* (see, e.g., 1095b19)—a slave's activity being a mere means for achieving purposes external to him. From this perspective, the objection we are considering thinks of children as needing an external slavedriver (motivations of 'bribe' or 'threat') until they have developed 'the capacity for deferred gratification', which is simply for them to have internalised this slavedriver.[2]

---

[2] This degraded conception of agency is deeply embedded in contemporary 'common-sense'. Alison Wolf, e.g., who is otherwise a fine debunker of many of the myths surrounding education, takes it

In his book *Freedom and Beyond*, Holt ends his lengthy discussion of these issues—of the creed of 'disagreeable hard work' and its instrumentalist assumptions—by quoting the last stanza of Robert Frost's poem "Two Tramps in Mud Time" (at Holt 1972, p. 117; quote corrected):

> But yield who will to their separation,
> My object in living is to unite
> My avocation with my vocation
> As my two eyes make one in sight.
> Only where love and need are one,
> And the work is play for mortal stakes,
> Is the deed ever really done,
> For Heaven and the future's sakes.

Instrumentalism presents us with a series of dichotomous oppositions: between 'effort' and 'pleasure', 'work' and 'leisure', 'work' and 'play'. As Frost and Holt both see, it is in human practices, done wholeheartedly, with love—making that activity for a time one's whole world—that these oppositions are overcome and transcended.

3.4 Objection #3: Noble Savages

Holt's position is based on a conception of the child as a kind of solitary 'noble savage'—who, if left free from social influences, will develop naturally and therefore authentically into a person who knows what they need to learn, and who possesses the virtues of inquiry. But this view is romantic and sentimentalised: children are social beings and need to learn in a social context; they cannot create the knowledge they need ab initio *out of their own experiences.*

The response to this objection is that the account it gives of Holt's position is a straw-man: Holt's views, properly understood, bear no relationship to this idea of the child as a kind of solitary 'noble savage'. However, the objection is a response to something in Holt, and it is worth drawing this out. This, in turn, will help to make sense of some important themes in Holt concerning the freedom of the learner and the nature of normative authority.

To begin with, it is worth pointing out that this objection is one that has actually been raised against Holt's views. Consider the following passage, from one of the very few scholarly articles directly discussing Holt's work:

> Holt has consistently, if not always explicitly, portrayed the child as a kind of noble savage representing authentic human nature, and associated social life as unnatural and corrupting and laissez faire individualism as the terrible but true state of nature. Holt's analyses of education have thus tended to be meditations on what he understands as an irreconcilable

---

for granted—asking her reader: "How much work do *you* do without either an immediate incentive or a deadline?" (2002, p. 289, n. 2), and clearly expecting the answer 'not much'. The word doing the work in Wolf's question is, of course, 'work'.

conflict between the natural individual and the oppressive and corrupting effects of organised social life. (Franzosa 1984, p. 231)

Another philosopher of education, Kathryn Morgan, raises a similar objection. Although she does not explicitly mention Holt, she claims that any form of 'open education' (in which she would include Holt's account of learning) must be based upon some version of Pestalozzi's "horticultural model" of the child. This model she describes as follows:

> First, the child is viewed primarily as a natural organism, that is, as a self-enclosed, self-regulating entity from which various needs, desires, interests, etc. emanate. Second, such interests, needs and desires are assumed to be intrinsic to, and uniquely individualised by the child at a pre-cultural or a-cultural stage of development. Third, the child thrives when he learns in accord with his natural rhythms and bents, the suggestion here being that these are present in a primitive, non-rational way and that they flow from the child. Fourth, all the learning that is thought desirable … can be found to be naturally motivated from within the child. (Morgan 1976, p. 25)

Both Franzosa and Morgan, then, suggest that Holt's view presupposes a dichotomous split between 'nature' and 'culture' (or 'organised social life'), which exist in 'irreconcilable conflict'. 'Nature' is authenticity, whilst 'culture' is the corruption of that authenticity. Given this framework, Holt's call for freedom in learning is then understood as involving the following argument: authenticity is the key good, and therefore children must be left as free from cultural or social influence as possible—for only with such freedom can they develop naturally, and hence authentically. Both Franzosa and Morgan then argue that such a view—a crudely lop-sided caricature of Rousseau—is deeply problematic on a number of grounds.

The position they ascribe to Holt is certainly problematic; indeed, it is preposterous. However, it bears almost no relation to the views he actually holds. Any careful reading of Holt's works will readily refute the claim that he believes anything like this, but the citation of a couple of relevant passages will suffice here. First, consider the following passage from *Teach Your Own*:

> Many people who quite like and enjoy children still seem to be in the grip of the old idea that in civilising them we have to give up or destroy some important part of them. To me that idea seems mistaken and harmful. … Many free schools, and some kindly and well-meaning parents, have suffered from the notion that there was something wild and precious in children that had to be preserved against the attacks of the world for as long as possible. Once we get free of this idea we will find our lives with children much easier and children themselves much happier. … basically [children] want to fit in, take part, and do right—that is, do as we do. (Holt 1981, p. 100)

And, a decade previously, in *Freedom and Beyond*, after a careful discussion of the "natural authority" of adults (Holt 1972, p. 64), Holt writes that,

> Man is a social, a cultural animal. Children sense around them this culture, this network of agreements, customs, habits, and rules binding the adults together. They want to understand it and be a part of it. They watch very carefully what people around them are doing and want to do the same. They want to do right, unless they become convinced they can't do right. (Holt 1972, p. 106)

As Holt's talk of 'agreements' and 'rules' makes clear, this social context is profoundly *normative*—it involves questions of what is right and wrong; correct and incorrect; appropriate and inappropriate; what is valuable and what is valueless; what matters and does not matter; what ought to be done and what ought not to be done. From this it follows that the social context involves *constraints*. Hence it is, as Holt points out, simply an obvious fact that, "As there is no life without structure, so there is no life without constraints" (Holt 1972, p. 25). Furthermore, this network of rules and agreements gives adults certain kinds of normative authority over children—the adults, for example, know the rules when the children may not. Therefore, as Holt writes, "we [adults] often *and rightly* intervene in the lives of children" (Holt 1972, p. 57; my emphasis).

This textual evidence demonstrates that Holt does not in the least believe (as Franzosa claims he does) that there is an "irreconcilable conflict between the natural individual and the oppressive and corrupting effects of organised social life". Holt does not think that there is a dichotomy between 'nature' and 'culture'. Nor does he hold that there is some pre-cultural or a-cultural notion of 'authenticity'. Nor does he hold the absurd view that children ought to be free from all social constraints. The objection's suggestion that Holt has some sentimentalised notion of the child as 'a kind of noble savage' is thus without merit.

However, we now need to consider whether a less extreme version of the objection has some truth to it; in particular, whether Holt believes—as Morgan suggests in the passage quoted above—that "all the learning that is thought desirable ... can be found to be naturally motivated from within the child". Whether this is a correct description of Holt's position or not, all depends upon how we take the words 'naturally' and 'from within'. As Morgan glosses it, it means that the child develops certain motivations (to learn) *independently* of any social influence or interaction. We have already seen that this cannot be Holt's view, for at no point does he speak of the individual-independent-of-society (there is no such thing), but only of the individual-in-her-social-context.

Holt's account certainly starts from the premise that almost all children, from a very young age, are profoundly moved by motivations of wonder, curiosity, and desires for competence in the world. He would suggest that this is simply a basic empirical fact about young human beings—and I see no reason to disagree. Infants and young children who lack these fundamental motivations—as in cases of brain injury, or severe deprivation—we see as profoundly damaged or disabled. This is not to claim, however, that the particular form that these motivations take is 'pre-cultural' or 'a-cultural'. For Holt, as we have seen, there is simply no point in talking about what the child might be like in a 'pre-cultural' or 'a-cultural' state, for to be human is to exist in a social context—in 'this network of agreements, customs, habits, and rules'. The question of what sorts of motivations and desires would exist in an infant raised by wolves may be of interest to some, but—at least until large numbers of our children are raised by wolves—it is not a question that we need to answer in order to think clearly about learning and education.

Hence, while Holt would perhaps agree that curiosity, wonder, and desires for competence exist 'naturally' in a child, the particular forms that those motivations

3.4 Objection #3: Noble Savages

and desires take will always be socially inflected. As we have seen, Holt argues that the 'best learning' occurs through undertaking practices for their own sake. Such autotelic activity begins with the child glimpsing something of the internal goods of a practice—some glimpse of the beauty or power of music; of the understanding produced by an explanation; of a piece of mathematics 'making sense'; of the challenges inherent in some sport or game, etc. But which practices the child is exposed to, and which ones will appear particularly valuable or significant, will all depend upon the social context in which the child lives. After all, children grow up in a world primarily structured by adult concerns and values, and they are deeply influenced by what activities the adults around them treat with seriousness of purpose, and what activities the adults consider contemptible or trivial.

At this point we can thus dispose of the suggestion that Holt's views consign adults to an entirely passive, or merely facilitative, role in respect to children and their desires. This is a common critique of 'child-centred' approaches to learning. Barrow, for example, has argued that 'radical educators' like Holt must, if they are to be true to their own principles, facilitate a child in pursuing *whatever* interests it has—suggesting that they are committed to the view that "if something interests somebody at a particular time it is for that reason a good thing for him to be doing it". He then raises the obvious counter-example: "Suppose a child has an interest in torturing cats. Shall I put information, sharp knives and a cat at his disposal?" (Barrow 1978, p. 103). R. S. Peters makes a similar argument, in more measured tones, remarking that,

> The child-centred teacher [has] the moral problem of choosing between letting children pursue their interests, which may be not at all in their interest, and getting them to pursue what is in their interest. (Peters 1966, pp. 35–6)

In sum, according to this line of criticism,

> There is … considerable implausibility in the suggestion that the aims of education are to be determined by considering the interests which children may actually be found to have at any given time. Why should interest in this sense be thought to be valuable, or even stable? (Dearden 1968, p. 20)

Barrow *et alii* are claiming that someone with a view like Holt's is confronted by a dilemma. Either—they claim—Holt must permit the child to pursue whatever interests she happens to have at the time, even when such pursuit may be harmful to the child, or he must allow that adults have a role in providing external motivations to push the child to pursue things that the child is not presently interested in—which would seem to be inconsistent with his broader views on the 'best learning'. However, this dilemma is generated by a false assumption. To begin with, Holt's position is not that whatever interests a child should be encouraged; rather, it is the converse of this, that whatever activities are encouraged should link to interests (desires, motivations) of the child. This erroneous understanding of what Holt is saying is further encouraged by the critics' failure to see the fundamental *continuity* (as emphasised in my reply to Objection #1) between the interests of children and those of adults. As discussed above, Holt suggests (with good reason) that all children—unless profoundly damaged—have deep motivations of wonder and curiosity, and desires for competence in the adult world. Given this, all children have the desires that are the starting points of a vast range of valuable human practices—and practices of inquiry in particular.

The objection that Holt presupposes some 'pre-cultural' or 'a-cultural' conception of the child, with its 'natural' motivations, that must be left uninfluenced by society in order to develop 'authentically', thus misses the mark. However, this objection is a response to something in Holt; it does not come from nowhere. What it is a response to, is Holt's repeated insistence on the importance of the *freedom* of the learner. As I have argued, this does not mean that the learner is free from the influence of human society, for only a wolf-child is free in *that* sense. It means that the learner learns best when she is able to engage in practices for their own sake rather than as efficient means to external ends. However, this raises the question of how engaging in a practice can yet be freedom. For, it might be thought, to engage in a practice is to be subject to the standards of excellence that constitute that practice. And, as Holt himself notes, to learn many practices may therefore entail engaging in activities that are,

> very tightly and rigidly structured. Any school of dance or the martial arts puts the students under the most intense and inflexible discipline. Watch students in a ballet or karate class at their work. As long as they stay in the class, they have no choices at all. Now, the instructor tells them, move like this. Arms move, legs move, all together. Go when I say go. Stop when I say stop. (Holt 1976, p. 21)

To understand how this 'most intense and inflexible discipline' can yet be freedom, it is worth looking more closely at how Holt's position compares to that of Rousseau, who faced a closely related problem in his philosophy of education. That is, to be clear, we need to compare Holt to the *real* Rousseau, rather than to a simple-minded caricature who talks of the child as a 'noble savage'.

Stated briefly, the problem that Rousseau undertakes to solve in his novel *Émile* is as follows. A child needs to be made a member of a society, and thus brought into a normative order (that 'network of agreements, customs, habits, and rules' of which Holt speaks). The usual way that this is done, Rousseau notes, is through the overt imposition of another's will on the child—the baby is swaddled, the young child is told what to do, and beaten if he does not do it. These impositions the child thinks of as injustices, and they inflame his *amour propre*—the concern that all humans possess for their right recognition as a fellow being in the eyes of others (cf. Rosenow 1980; Dent 1988). Over time, this produces an adult who suffers from a profound internal conflict—a fragmentation of the self—in that his desires will tend to run in opposition to what is required of him by social norms (thus, his duties, obligations, and the like). As Rousseau writes,

> He who in the civil order wants to preserve the primacy of the sentiments of nature does not know what he wants. Always in contradiction with himself, always floating between his inclinations and his duties, he will never be either man or citizen. (Rousseau 1979, p. 40)

For such people, neither freedom nor sincerity is possible; they can neither wholeheartedly do what they desire to do, nor wholeheartedly avow what they believe (cf. Williams 2002, Chap. 5).

In *Émile*, Rousseau narrates an imagined solution to this problem: an education that will produce a genuinely integrated human being, able to take a place in society as a citizen in the true sense. Rousseau's solution is to have Émile's tutor systematically, but surreptitiously, manipulate the boy's environment. In this environment, the child acts howsoever he wishes and experiences the consequences of his actions; however, the child experiences those consequences as if they followed *naturally* from his acts. That is to say, the tutor so arranges Émile's environment that, to the child, the consequences of his acts appear simply as the causal effects of those acts, with no sense of an alien will being imposed on him. To take just one example, when Émile breaks the window of his bedroom, the room is cold when he tries to sleep. The child does not perceive this as a *punishment* (which would imply the imposition of another's will), but simply as the natural, necessary consequence of his action.

The tutor's intention in this is for Émile to modify his own desires—just as a person, having once touched a hot stove, no longer desires to do so—so as to fit with the normative requirements of society. However, this modification is seen by the child as his own choice, taken in response to natural necessities, rather than occurring through the imposition of another's will. The process therefore does not inflame the child's sense of injustice. Rousseau thus writes,

> Let him always believe he is master, and let it always be you who are. There is no subjection so perfect as that which keeps the appearance of freedom. Thus the will itself is made captive. The poor child who knows nothing, who can do nothing, who has no learning, is he not at your mercy? Do you not dispose, with respect to him, of everything which surrounds him? Are you not the master of affecting him as you please? Are not his labors, his games, his pleasures, his pains, all in your hands without his knowing it? Doubtless he ought to do only what he wants; but he ought to want only what you want him to do. He ought not to make a step without your having foreseen it; he ought not to open his mouth without your knowing what he is going to say. (Rousseau 1979, p. 120)

Rousseau argues that this manipulation (what we might call a behavioural conditioning) produces an integrated psyche whose desires have been shaped to correspond to social norms. Those social norms are thus perceived by that psyche as necessities and as 'natural', rather than as the imposition of an alien will. As Émile remarks at the end of the book, "I would want only what is and therefore would never have to struggle against destiny" (Rousseau 1979, p. 472). Émile, in other words, has become a true citizen, who wholeheartedly desires to do what he ought to do.

Before relating this back to Holt, it is worth noting how Aristotle's concept of virtue provides a solution to a structurally parallel problem. As discussed in the previous chapter, a virtue relates to the will, in that to ascribe a virtue to a person is, in part, to ascribe to them certain sorts of desires and motivations. The virtuous person, that is, is someone who not only *knows* the right act to perform in the circumstances, but also *wants* to perform that act. In this way, in Aristotle's account, the virtues give unity to the psyche—it is through possession of the virtues that the agent will experience no internal conflicts between her desires and the felt demands of social norms.

Now, Holt is not operating on as large a metaphysical canvas as these philosophers, but he faces a similar problem in his own domain of learning. As noted above,

Rousseau sought to resolve the problem of how to bring children into a society (a normative order) without the overt imposition of another's will. The solution given in *Émile* may not be directly coercive, but there is no doubt that it is profoundly manipulative. In contrast to Rousseau, Holt's main focus is not with children's relation to broader social norms, but he is concerned with their entry into the normative orders of practices. That is, Holt's question is how children can come to accept the normative demands of practices (such as mathematics, reading, music, and so on) without the imposition of an educator's will. In other words, how is freedom in learning possible?

Holt's solution to this question contains a significant conceptual advance over Rousseau. For Rousseau, the only way for an agent to come to accept a normative demand is by way of the imposition of another's will. That is why the only alternative that Rousseau sees to the *overt* imposition of that will, is its *covert* imposition; hence the tutor's deceptive manipulation of Émile's environment. Holt, however, distinguishes between two kinds of what he terms 'discipline'. On the one hand, there is what he terms the "Discipline of Superior Force" (Holt 1972, p. 107), which corresponds to Rousseau's notion of the imposition of another's will. Unlike Rousseau, Holt sees nothing wrong with such coercion per se—writing that, "There is bound to be some of this in a child's life. Living as we do surrounded by things that can hurt children, or that children can hurt, we cannot avoid it" (Holt 1972, 107). But, as we have seen, Holt argues that there is no place for the exercise of such 'superior force' in learning—in coercing people into learning one thing rather than another. There is, however, a place in learning for *another* kind of discipline, Holt's term for which is the "Discipline of Culture, of Society, of What People Really Do" (Holt 1972, p. 106). This concept—which is not visible to Rousseau—allows Holt to resolve the question of how freedom in learning is possible, for it allows us to make good sense of the idea of an agent's *willing submission* to norms.

In order to understand this, consider Holt's two paradigm examples of learning, to which he returns again and again in his works: the infant's acquisition of language, and learning to play a musical instrument. In neither case, does it make the least sense to think of the learner as beginning *ab initio*, and inventing this knowledge from the ground up. As Holt writes,

> We do not ask or expect a child to invent the wheel starting from scratch. He doesn't have to. The wheel has been invented. It is out there, in front of him. ... The whole culture is out there. (Holt 1983, p. 290)

When one undertakes a human practice—such as beginning to speak a language; beginning to play the cello—one is confronting a pre-existing normative order, deeply informed by traditions, and exemplified in existing activities by current practitioners. That is, the infant cannot 'speak' howsoever she wishes (if she wishes to be understood; that is, if she wishes to *speak*). Nor can she simply 'play music' howsoever she wishes, for what she does in such a case will then be *noise*-making, not *music*-making. In other words, the practice confronts the learner like an objective reality—a *world*. As Iris Murdoch puts it,

> If I am learning, for instance, Russian, I am confronted by an authoritative structure which commands my respect. The task is difficult and the goal is distant and perhaps never entirely

attainable. My work is a progressive revelation of something which exists independently of me. Attention is rewarded by a knowledge of reality. Love of Russian leads me away from myself towards something alien to me, something which my consciousness cannot take over, swallow up, deny or make unreal. (Murdoch 1997, p. 373)

Hence, Murdoch argues, free agency is best thought of as a willing "obedience" to such an authoritative structure, rather than as "unimpeded movement" (Murdoch 1997, p. 331). That is, in the terms used here, undertaking a practice involves a submission to the internal standards of excellence that constitute that practice; for the road to mastery begins with apprenticeship. This is, in Holt's words, a submission to an 'intense and inflexible discipline'—of what is demanded by excellence in that practice. But this submission is *willing*, because it involves the agent coming to grasp the internal goods of that practice—that is, grasping them *as* goods, and hence as worth pursuing for themselves.

Holt would thus reject the interminable educational debate between, on the one hand, those who insist that, in learning, children must 'construct' their own understanding, and, on the other hand, those who insist that learning involves the 'transmission' of a culturally-shared understanding. This acrimonious split between 'constructivist' and 'transmission' models of learning is, from Holt's perspective, based upon a false dichotomy. Through engaging in practices one progressively grasps their internal standards of excellence, which are in no way personal or private to an individual. On the contrary, they are, as Murdoch writes, a 'revelation of something which exists independently of me'. Such conceptions of excellence have developed historically, and in many cases are embedded in the structures of institutions. To this extent, the claims of the 'transmission model' are entirely correct. However, the 'constructivists' are also correct in emphasising that the individual agency of the learner is crucial to learning. This is because in grasping the internal goods of a practice, one is making those standards of excellence *one's own*.

To make clearer what I mean by this latter point, consider the following. We can distinguish at least two senses of the word 'learn' (cf. Burnyeat 1980, pp. 74–6). I can learn-in-the-superficial-sense that something is the case simply by being told it is so, and taking it on trust. I can, for example, learn from a trusted authority that Gödel's incompleteness theorems prove that arithmetic cannot be finitely axiomatised. However, let us suppose I know nothing of formal logic, and thus those proofs are unreadable by me. In such a case, I have learned something, but I have not made the understanding (of what Gödel's proofs achieve) *my own*. To make such understanding my own is to learn, as it were, to *see* that something is the case *off my own bat*. In the imagined example, this is for the validity and power of a passage of logical reasoning to become *seeable by me*—for me to be able to read the proofs, follow Gödel's reasoning, and see for myself what they prove. To use another example, it is one thing to learn (by reading it somewhere, or being told) that Miles Davis is a great jazz musician; it is quite another for my education in jazz to progress to the point where Davis's greatness has become *hearable by me*, as I listen to 'Kind of Blue'. When I can do this, I have learned to make the understanding my own; I am grasping the internal goods of the practice; they have become goods *for me*.

This is thus how Holt resolves the problem of freedom in learning. Through engagement in a practice, the internal goods of that practice are progressively revealed to the agent and made her own. Such engagement is, therefore, not the imposition of another's will on the agent, but a process of the agent's *self*-transformation. This is clearly expressed by MacIntyre, who contrasts the model in which

> the educator takes her or himself not only to know more, but also to know best, ... to know what is genuinely good for others, something that they do not themselves know. Hence educators suppose themselves to be entitled to impose upon others *their* conception of the good. (MacIntyre 1994, p. 287)

This is the coercive or manipulative model of education that Holt rejects—it is, in his words, "the ugly and antihuman business of people-shaping" (Holt 1976, p. 4). It involves the imposition of another's will (justified, of course, on the paternalistic grounds that the educators 'know best … what is genuinely good for others'). In contrast to this, MacIntyre writes, there is

> quite another kind of practice, one such that those engaged in it transform themselves and educate themselves through their own self-transformative activity, coming to understand their good as the good internal to that activity. (MacIntyre 1994, p. 287)

As should now be clear, this is the sort of 'doing' and 'best learning' of which Holt speaks. Through such activity, engaged in for its own sake, the self is transformed. The agent enters a normative order, not through coercion or manipulation by another, but through her willing submission to the internal standards of excellence of the practice. Her submission is willing, because through that activity those standards progressively reveal themselves to her as goods—as valuable, significant, and worth pursuing, in themselves (not simply as a means to some external end). And this is why engagement with practices is, as MacIntyre writes, a self-transformative activity; a deep expression of agency.

Despite its emphasis on the freedom of the learner, Holt's position can thus be seen, in an important sense, as an *inversion* of a 'constructivist' and 'child-centred' approach. Knowledge is not shaped to the learner's desires and experience; on the contrary, the learner *shapes herself* to the knowledge, by transforming her will. Through progressively grasping the internal goods of the practices—as she develops the virtues of those practices—her sense of what is valuable, significant, and worth doing, is transformed. In other words, through engaging in practices, through her own pursuit of their goods, the learner *makes herself* into a mathematician, a musician, a joiner, a chess-player, a speaker of a language, etc.

3.5 Objection #4: Teachers and Teaching

Holt's position is faced with a dilemma: either he is suggesting that teachers and teaching have no role at all to play in learning, which is absurd; or he is saying that teachers and teaching do have a legitimate role, in which case his 'critique of education' is far less radical than it is claimed to be.

3.5 Objection #4: Teachers and Teaching

In order to answer this objection, more clarity is needed on how Holt's views have the conceptual space to provide, without inconsistency, a legitimate role for teachers and explicit teaching. To begin with, as should be clear from the previous discussions in this chapter, Holt does not think that learning is intrinsically or essentially a solitary pursuit, nor does he hold the view that the learner must construct knowledge *ab initio*. Even when Holt's focus is on the individual child, exploring the world in her own way, without direct assistance of any kind, this is not a view of the child as a sort of Robinson Crusoe. For the world she is exploring is a deeply *social* one: a world of normative order; of culture, communities, and human practices; of people engaged together in various activities. Holt is thus clear that learning involves, in many cases, learning from others. After all, he writes, it is just obvious that "you would be unlikely to learn any complicated and difficult human activity without drawing heavily on the experience of those who know it better" (Holt 1972, pp. 108–9). There are many ways of learning from others; or, as he puts it in the subtitle of *Instead of Education*, there are many ways "to help people do things better".

There is little doubt that Holt's views have been strongly associated with a particular way in which adults can help children learn, or 'do things better'. This is the thought that (particularly very young) children can best learn by being given access to a rich and stimulating human world, and then allowed to explore it in their own way, with no, or very few, episodes of explicit teaching. As he writes in the final paragraph of *Learning All the Time*:

> We can best help children learn, not by deciding what we think they should learn and thinking of ingenious ways to teach it to them, but by making the world, so far as we can, accessible to them, paying serious attention to what they do, answering their questions—if they have any—and helping them explore the things they are most interested in. (Holt 1989, p. 162)

Or, as he puts this thought in *How Children Learn*,

> Keeping their curiosity 'well supplied with food' *doesn't* mean feeding them, or telling them what they have to feed themselves. It means putting within their reach the widest possible variety and quantity of good food—like taking them to a supermarket with no junk food in it (if we can imagine such a thing). (Holt 1983, p. 233)

This sort of free exploration in the world is sometimes thought to be the essential and appropriate method of 'unschooling', and there is no doubt that it is an approach that Holt strongly emphasises. One reason for this is that such emphasis is an antidote to the disempowering thought—implicit in much of the practice of our official educational institutions—that "everything, however trivial, must be deliberately taught" (Holt 1971, p. 72). However, if we read the above passages in the broader context of his work as a whole, it is clear that Holt recognises a huge variety of ways in which people can learn from one another as being consistent with his views about learning and education.

Holt's works—in particular, *Instead of Education* (especially Chaps. 7–8), and the many examples given in *Teach Your Own*—discuss a wide range of ways in which people can help others 'do things better'. As just remarked, he discusses the many ways in which children can learn by doing things without any explicit kinds of teaching. For example: through solitary activities, with adults simply being there as a supportive presence, able to answer questions or offer advice when requested; through cooperative play and fantasy with other children; through working with others at real-world activities (by assisting with cooking meals, shopping for groceries, gardening, etc.). However, along with these expected forms of 'unschooling' approaches, Holt also discusses in many places various forms of explicit teaching, and the legitimate role that teachers can play in the 'best learning'. Hence, it is not the case that Holt's position rules out teaching and teachers per se. Rather, as he repeatedly remarks, "It all depends on the spirit in which this is done" (Holt 1981, p. 154). So, to make sense of how Holt can consistently hold this view, and thus answer the objection, we need an account of just what this right 'spirit' is.

The answer to this question comes if we examine a passage in *Instead of Education*, in which Holt is discussing a particularly authoritarian form of teaching, namely, training in classical ballet. Such teaching—rigid in sequencing and structure, with no room for individual choice—is a world away from the sort of 'free exploration' and 'learning through play' with which Holt and 'unschooling' is typically associated, yet Holt sees it as entirely legitimate. The reason why Holt thinks such teaching is compatible with his views about 'best learning' and the freedom of the learner comes in the following passage, where he writes that,

> the tasks that the dancing master gives the student make sense. *The student can see, and feel in his body, the connection between these beginning movements and the full skill and art he wants to master.* Indeed, the greatest dancers begin their work every day with the same simple movements the student is trying to learn to do. (Holt 1976, p. 59; my emphasis)

In contrast to this, too often in the kind of teaching that is characteristic of 'education' (in Holt's sense of the word), "The child cannot see any connection between the things he is told to do, and the goal he at first wanted to reach" (Holt 1976, p. 59). These remarks give us the criterion that distinguishes good ways of helping people to learn, from harmful ways: the teacher must so act that the internal goods of the practice remain in sight for the learner. Or, to put this criterion in the way that Holt states it later in *Instead of Education*, the 'doing' must remain the project of the learner, rather than becoming the project of the teacher (Holt 1976, p. 102).

This is another way of putting the point that was discussed in the previous chapter, when we looked at Holt's account of the role in music-making of exercises such as scales, arpeggios, and the like. The key point reached in that discussion was that the agent should not think of such exercises in instrumental terms, as efficient means to certain ends. Rather, such exercises should be thought of as organic parts of a unified practice of music-making—that is, as oriented to a pursuit of the internal goods of that practice. In the same way, Holt is emphasising that the study of classical ballet is composed of activities that the student can see as directly connected to the internal goods of the practice. In this way, the ballet student's study, whilst rigidly sequenced and structured by the teacher, can be seen by the student as an organic part of his (the student's) engagement in the practice of ballet, oriented to its internal goods. Hence, recalling the discussion of the previous objection above, the student can see his own activity as a student not as a submission to the will of the *individual* who is his teacher, but as a submission to the demands of *ballet*—and thus as part of

3.5 Objection #4: Teachers and Teaching

his own self-transformation into a ballet dancer. That is, although the teaching is authoritarian, the student can grasp the exercise of that authority as embodying the standards of excellence of the practice, rather than it simply appearing to him as the more-or-less arbitrary will of the individual who is the teacher. All of this, of course, presupposes that the student has *chosen* to undertake the practice of ballet for its own sake—in pursuit of its internal goals. But, given such a choice, there is a clear and legitimate role for explicit teaching.

However, Holt is also clear that this sort of explicit teaching carries dangers and temptations with it. As he writes, "teaching is a very strong medicine, which like all strong medicines can quickly and easily turn into a poison" (Holt 1978, p. 209). As I have discussed, teaching (even of the most authoritarian kind) is legitimate so long as the learner retains the locus of agency—that is to say, so long as the activities engaged in under the teacher's direction can be grasped by the learner as organic parts of her own 'project', or unified engagement in a practice. The danger of explicit teaching lies in the fact that it is all too easy for the locus of agency to shift to the teacher. This is particularly the case when the teacher-student relationship is strongly marked by other power dynamics, such as when the learner is a child and the teacher an adult. This shift of agency occurs when the student can no longer grasp his own activity as submission to the internal goods of the practice; that is, as Holt puts it, when the student can no longer "see any connection between the things he is told to do, and the goal he at first wanted to reach". Rather, from the student's perspective it has become submission to the *will* of another—motivated by external incentives and disincentives. To use Holt's terms, it is no longer genuine 'doing'; instead, it is now 'education'. When such a shift of agency occurs, the teacher thus becomes an *educator*: someone who, in the words of Alasdair MacIntyre in the passage quoted above, "know[s] what is genuinely good for others, something that they do not themselves know".

As discussed in the previous chapter, this form of teaching, in which the agency lies with the teacher rather than with the student, promotes various vices of practices. In particular, it tends to promote what we might term the vices of disempowerment and alienation: passivity, helplessness, intellectual cowardice, and the like. As Holt writes,

> Most of our schools convey to children a very powerful message, that they are stupid, worthless, untrustworthy, unfit to make even the smallest decisions about their own lives or learning. (Holt 1970, p. 56)

This is *alienation* because, by its very form, teaching of this nature tends to encourage the student to think that she is unable to be the agent of her own transformation, but must instead be transformed by the hands of another—the teacher. In this way, the student comes to think that the teacher is the source of something that is, in fact, her own capacity. At this point, it is worth recalling a fable told by the great anarchist thinker Errico Malatesta, who asks us to imagine that,

> a man who had had his limbs bound from his birth, but had nevertheless found out how to hobble about, might attribute to the very hands that bound him his ability to move, while,

> on the contrary, they would be diminishing and paralyzing the muscular energy of his limbs. (Malatesta 2013, p. 2)

In this fable, Malatesta was talking of how we come to think of the capacity of organisation as something that is provided by government (without which we would exist in chaos), when in fact (he argues) government is entirely parasitic upon the ordinary human capacity for self-organisation and mutual aid. Holt's views run parallel to Malatesta's thought: education, Holt argues, encourages us to think that valuable learning is a product of teaching; that we can learn anything significant only by being taught according to another's conception of the good; that any learning we gain for ourselves, outside of credential-granting institutions, is therefore trivial and worthless. Yet, Holt is saying, all such instrumentalised learning is only a 'hobbling' of our deep capacities for self-reliance, self-organisation, and self-transformation.

Holt in fact suggests that not only is teaching a 'strong medicine' that must be used sparingly if it is not to work against the student's 'best learning', but also that it contains within it something potentially corrupting of the *teacher*. In *Instead of Education*, Holt approvingly cites Illich's angry disavowal of the role (addressed to an audience member at a symposium): "Please sit down. I am *not* your teacher" (quoted in Holt 1976, p. 108). And in a 1978 letter to Illich, Holt writes that,

> I find myself thinking, saying, and writing more and more in recent months that the very idea of a full-time teacher is deeply mistaken, that whatever teaching we do we ought to do as an incidental part of the rest of our life. I hardly think any more that it's possible to be a full-time teacher, I don't care [in] what kind of school or institutional setting, without corrupting the relationships between oneself and other people. (Holt 1990, pp. 215–6)

This remark is certainly a refreshing change from the treacly, self-congratulatory cant that tends to surround discussions of teaching ('the most important profession in the world', etc.). A full discussion of the sorts of ethical temptations that reside in teaching is far beyond the scope of this essay, but I will conclude with a very brief consideration of the thinking that may lie behind Holt's remark, and how it relates to his broader views on learning.

To make sense of what Holt is saying here, consider what is involved in teaching a practice. What makes a person's activity *teaching* is, in part, the intention animating it. And, in the words of Paul Hirst, "The intention of all teaching activities is that of bringing about learning" (Hirst 1975, p. 168). The danger inherent in this intentional structure, is that of one's words and actions *qua* teacher becoming tools that are used in order to bring about a certain future outcome (that the student learn such-and-such). That is, *qua* teacher one's relationships with one's students, and with one's own practice, are necessarily marked by a constant temptation to instrumentalism. If I am teaching a practice and start to consider my own activity primarily as a means to produce certain effects on others (such as to produce certain 'learning outcomes') I have thereby lost sight myself of the internal goods of that practice. I am now 'modelling' the practice for others, rather than engaging in it wholeheartedly for the sake of its internal goods. When this occurs, my words and actions *qua* teacher cease to bear an integral relation to my own grasp of the practice.

3.5 Objection #4: Teachers and Teaching

As a contrast to help to make this point clearer, consider the character of Socrates, as Plato presents him. It is a cliché that Socrates is one of the 'great teachers' of history. But, in an important sense, Socrates is *not* a teacher. He himself states this in the *Apology* as clearly as anyone can:

> I have never set up as any man's teacher, but if anyone, young or old, is eager to hear me conversing and carrying out my private mission, I never grudge him the opportunity; nor do I charge a fee for talking to him, and refuse to talk without one. I am ready to answer questions for rich and poor alike, and I am equally ready if anyone prefers to listen to me and answer my questions. If any given one of these people becomes a good citizen or a bad one, I cannot fairly be held responsible, since I have never promised or imparted any teaching to anybody, and if anyone asserts that he has ever learned or heard from me privately anything which was not open to everyone else, you may be quite sure that he is not telling the truth. (Plato 1961, 33a–b)

I can, of course, *learn from* Socrates—and Plato clearly wants us to do that. But Socrates never speaks and acts with the intention of producing learning in others; he does not view his own words and acts as instruments in this way.[3] Indeed, it is a core part of his critique of the Sophists and the rhetoricians that *they* view their words as instruments in just such a way, and that this is an aspect of their commitment to a reductionist view of the human being and the human good. It is precisely the heart of Socrates's integrity that he does not use his words manipulatively, as tools or instruments. Rather, all his words and actions express his sense of his own life; they *are* the activity of him living 'the examined life'; he stakes and commits himself with every word that he speaks. To put this another way, Socrates does not set out to *teach* his hearers and interlocutors. Instead, he sets out to seek the truth in dialogue with them—to engage in the practice of *philosophy* with them, and strive wholeheartedly in pursuit of its internal goods. That is to say, Socrates is not setting out to 'educate' people; his philosophical discussions are not 'learning activities', engaged in with one eye on the 'learning outcomes' to be produced by them; he does not intend his actions as 'models' for those around him. Socrates, in Holt's terms, is engaged in genuine 'doing' rather than 'educating'—and just this is why he is worth learning from.

3.6 Objection #5: Utopianism

Holt's views are utopian and therefore entirely unhelpful. Our society is simply not structured in a way that is favourable for the 'best learning', and there is no realistic chance it will become so. Hence, Holt's views are useless for helping us devise, here and now, practical strategies for positive change. That is, his views fail to help us to answer the question 'What is to be done?'.

This is a crucial objection, and it is what I will discuss in the final chapter of this book.

---

[3] This point has not been well-understood in the literature on Socrates's claim. It is missed entirely, e.g., in Mintz 2013.

References

Aristotle. (1984). *Nichomachean ethics* (W. D. Ross, Trans.). In J. Barnes (Ed.), *The complete works of Aristotle: The revised Oxford translation*. Princeton, NJ: Princeton University Press.
Barrow, R. (1978). *Radical education: A critique of freeschooling and deschooling*. Oxford: Martin Robertson.
Borgmann, A. (1984). *Technology and the character of contemporary life: A philosophical inquiry*. Chicago, IL: University of Chicago Press.
Brewer, T. (2009). *The retrieval of ethics*. Oxford: Oxford University Press.
Burnyeat, M. F. (1980). Aristotle on learning to be good. In A. O. Rorty (Ed.), *Essays on Aristotle's Ethics* (pp. 69–92). Berkeley, CA: University of California Press.
Dearden, R. F. (1968). *The philosophy of primary education: An introduction*. London: Routledge and Kegan Paul.
Dent, N. (1988). *Rousseau: An introduction to his psychological, social and political theory*. Oxford: Basil Blackwell.
Elster, J. (1985). *Making sense of Marx*. Cambridge: Cambridge University Press.
Elster, J. (1986). Self-realization in work and politics: The Marxist conception of the good life. *Social Philosophy and Policy, 3*(2), 97–126.
Franzosa, S. D. (1984). The best and wisest parent: A critique of John Holt's philosophy of education. *Urban Education, 19*(3), 227–44.
Gutmann, A. (1999). *Democratic education* (revised ed.). Princeton, NJ: Princeton University Press.
Hirst, P. (1975). What is teaching? In R. S. Peters (Ed.), *The philosophy of education* (pp. 163–77). London: Routledge and Kegan Paul.
Holt, J. (1970). *What do I do Monday?* New York: E. P. Dutton and Co.
Holt, J. (1971). Big bird, meet Dick and Jane: A critique of Sesame Street. *Atlantic Monthly, 227*(5), 72–8.
Holt, J. (1972). *Freedom and beyond*. Harmondsworth: Penguin.
Holt, J. (1974). *Escape from childhood: The needs and rights of children*. New York: E. P. Dutton and Co.
Holt, J. (1976). *Instead of education*. New York: E. P. Dutton and Co.
Holt, J. (1978). *Never too late: My musical life story*. New York: Merloyd Lawrence.
Holt, J. (1981). *Teach your own: A hopeful path for education*. Liss, Hants: Lighthouse Books.
Holt, J. (1982). *How children fail* (revised ed.). New York: Merloyd Lawrence.
Holt, J. (1983). *How children learn* (revised ed.). London: Penguin.
Holt, J. (1989). *Learning all the time*. New York: Merloyd Lawrence.
Holt, J. (1990). Letter to Ivan Illich, 5/24/78. In S. Sheffer, (Ed.). (1990). *A life worth living: Selected letters of John Holt* (pp. 213–8). Columbus, OH: Ohio State University Press.
Kant, I. (2007). Lectures on pedagogy (R. B. Louden, Trans.) In *Anthropology, history, and education* (G. Zöller & R. B. Louden, Eds.). Cambridge: Cambridge University Press.
Mach, E. (1903). *Populär-Wissenschaftliche Vorlesungen*. Leipzig: Johann Ambrosius Barth.
MacIntyre, A. (1994). The *Theses on Feuerbach*: A road not taken. In C. C. Gould & R. S. Cohen, (Eds.), *Artifacts, representations and social practice* (pp. 277–90). Dordrecht: Kluwer.
Malatesta, E. (2013). *Anarchy*. Saint Louis, MO: Dialectics.
Marx, K. (1973). *Grundrisse: Introduction to the critique of political economy* (M. Nicolaus, Trans.). Harmondsworth: Penguin.
Matthews, G. B. (1992). *Dialogues with children*. Cambridge, MA: Harvard University Press.
Matthews, G. B. (1994). *The philosophy of childhood*. Cambridge, MA: Harvard University Press.
Mintz, A. I. (2013). Why did Socrates Deny that he was a teacher? Locating Socrates among the new educators and the traditional education in Plato's Apology of Socrates. *Educational Philosophy and Theory, 46*(7), 735–47.
Morgan, K. (1976). Children, bonsai trees, and open education. *The Journal of Educational Thought, 10*(1), 22–33.

References

Murdoch, I. (1997). The sovereignty of good over other concepts. *Existentialists and mystics: Writings on philosophy and literature* (pp. 363–85). London: Chatto and Windus.

Orff, C., & Keetman, G. (1950). *Musik für Kinder: In Fünftonraum* (Vol. 1). Mainz: Schott.

Peters, R. S. (1966). *Ethics and education*. London: George Allen and Unwin.

Plato. (1961). *Collected dialogues* (E. Hamilton & H. Cairns, Eds.). Princeton, NJ: Princeton University Press.

Ramsey, F. P. (1928). A mathematical theory of saving. *The Economic Journal, 38*(152), 543–59.

Rosenow, E. (1980). Rousseau's *Émile*: An anti-utopia. *British Journal of Educational Studies, 28*(3), 212–24.

Rousseau, J-J. (1979). *Émile: Or on education* (A. Bloom, Trans.). New York: Basic Books.

Ryle, G. (1990). *The concept of mind*. London: Penguin.

Ryle, G. (2009). Pleasure. *Collected essays 1929–1968* (pp. 339–48). London: Routledge.

Williams, B. (2002). *Truth and truthfulness: An essay in genealogy*. Princeton, NJ: Princeton University Press.

Wolf, A. (2002). *Does education matter? Myths about education and economic growth*. London: Penguin.

Chapter 4
What Is to Be Done?

… we have created a world of dynamic machines or tools and institutions, and static men; or living tools and dead men. (Holt 1990a, p. 149)

4.1 Introduction

It is now time to turn from theory to a brief consideration of practice—to ask the question, if something like the analysis given in the preceding chapters is correct, then what, if anything, does it demand that we *do*? At the end of chapter one, it was pointed out that, considered analytically, Holt's works consist of three main components. First, they contain a positive or constructive account of what he considers the 'best learning', the sorts of conditions that promote such learning, and the sorts of conditions that are hostile to it. Secondly, they contain a critique of education, which is justified by appeal to the foregoing account of 'best learning'. And thirdly, they contain a range of practical strategies, aimed at mitigating the problems of education (especially compulsory schooling) and maximising the opportunity of acquiring the 'best learning'. This third component was of great significance to Holt. Although there is a sense in which Holt's work is 'utopian', in that it criticises some foundational cultural assumptions and envisages a possible society that exists nowhere, he is, at the same time, a deeply practical, realistic thinker. He does not offer airy plans for grand social reconstruction, addressed to nobody in particular; rather, he tries to answer the question of what can be done by us, here and now. In the words of one of his book titles, he wants to answer the question: What do I do Monday?

As was remarked in the first chapter, Holt is best known today as a key figure in the history of the homeschooling movement. For this reason, this concluding chapter will focus particularly on his proposal that homeschooling is the best practical strategy for providing a context in which children can maximise their opportunities of achieving the 'best learning'. I have no intention of offering a detailed assessment or discussion of homeschooling in general—an area on which there is a substantial literature, both scholarly and non-scholarly (for a recent, systematic survey, see Rothermel 2015). The focus here will be much more restricted and specific: looking at how homeschooling, as a practical strategy, relates to Holt's views on learning and education.

To understand Holt's recommendation of homeschooling, it is important to situate it within the context of his developing thought about practical strategies. I have argued in previous chapters that a particular conception of the 'best learning' is present in all his works. This conception was deepened and clarified over the course of Holt's writing, but in fundamentals it remains the same from his first book, *How Children Fail*, through to the posthumous *Learning All the Time*. However, over this period the practical strategies he recommends in his books shift substantially. In Holt's early works (*How Children Fail* through to *What do I do Monday?*) the strategies are largely pedagogical, aimed at teachers who wish to make their classes more friendly to learner-directed learning. By the time of *Instead of Education* (1976) Holt has largely given up on the idea that the 'best learning' can be achieved in any real way within the context of compulsory schooling. The strategies he proposes in this work thus shift to what might be termed, with a nod to anarchist thought, 'mutual aid solutions'—the building of non-hierarchical counter-institutions and resources that can promote learning outside of the official educational system. Finally, in *Teach Your Own* (1981), Holt extends this mutualism to the building of a community of homeschoolers, offering detailed practical advice on all aspects of what is involved in withdrawing a child from compulsory schooling.

I will examine each of these three proposed strategies in a little more detail in a moment, but to begin with, this summary allows me to clarify an important preliminary point. In order to answer the question 'what is to be done?', it is of crucial importance to specify the intended *agent* of this doing—or, equivalently, the audience being addressed by these practical recommendations and exhortations. Holt's practical strategies are addressed to particular groups of people at a particular time and place. The particular time and place is, of course, the USA in the 1970s and early 1980s. The particular groups he aims at change with the shifts in his proposed strategies. The early, pedagogical strategies are, obviously enough, aimed at teachers who shared Holt's views about learning, and were looking for approaches that could be used within the classroom to maximise the learner's freedom. The later strategies are increasingly aimed at parents and children, who shared Holt's views and were looking for ways of escaping the educational system altogether. Holt's practical strategies are thus aimed at providing suggestions for action that can realistically be implemented (on Monday!) by agents who are relatively powerless in relation to the education system.

In this way, Holt stands in stark contrast to too many books on educational theory, which tend to offer vague prescriptions addressed to a mythical agent—namely, "an all-powerful and all-benevolent policy-making apparatus" (Ferguson 1990, p. 280). Consider, for example, the following passage (taken more or less at random) from Amy Gutmann's *Democratic Education*:

4.1 Introduction

> ... states should take greater responsibility for financing primary education or for making more effective use of existing resources; the content of education should be reoriented towards teaching students the skills of democratic deliberation; and the federal government should give local schools more money for educating handicapped children. (Gutmann 1999, p. 171)

Here is a forest of impersonal *should's*, in which nobody in particular is being addressed. There are no details of precise policies that could be used to implement any of these *should's*, nor how political alliances could be built to bring them about, nor any consideration of the sorts of difficult compromises that real implementation would involve. And, of course, for all Guttman's talk of 'democracy', all these *should's* are implicitly authoritarian. For these recommendations are not addressed to teachers, parents, or students, nor do they leave any room for their active involvement, other than to be the passive *objects* of such top-down policy-making—in which they will find themselves being variously *resourced*, *used* (more effectively!), *taught*, and *educated*. This authoritarianism, along with the high-altitude, abstract refusal to tangle in the messy world of real action is, unfortunately, all too typical of the 'practical' conclusions of a lot of educational theory.[1] Holt's own practical strategies, with their concrete details, their genuine practical wisdom, and their desire to address 'ordinary people', are a world away from *this* sort of utopianism.

4.2 Shifting Strategies

As noted, in his early works Holt's practical strategies were addressed primarily to an audience of like-minded teachers in the US school system. These were teachers who were looking for ways of making their classrooms much more 'child-centred', in the context of the authoritarian nature of typical US public schools at this time. Holt's early works are thus rich collections of very detailed pedagogical techniques and suggestions for connecting learning more closely to the motivations of children, and bringing more 'real' activities into their learning. They include suggestions for setting up contexts which will encourage children to explore literacy and numeracy in more self-directed ways; approaches to explaining arithmetical concepts in ways that connect more closely to children's understanding; lists of useful teaching resources and where to obtain them; advice on how to deal with the external demands of the schooling system (e.g., grading) in ways that will render them less harmful to learning.

Holt's views about the best practical strategies have shifted dramatically by the time he wrote *Instead of Education*. As its title indicates, Holt is no longer discussing how people working *inside* the education system can mitigate its negative impacts on learning, but on how learning can best occur *outside* of official educational systems altogether. This shift in approach reflects the belief that,

---

[1] All too typical, in fact, of much contemporary political philosophy in general. For an excellent critique of this approach, see Geuss (2008).

> constructive change in human affairs does not come about through people clashing with and reforming old institutions, but by their setting up new institutions which because they meet more important human needs gradually displace the old. (Holt 1990b, pp. 60–1)

This radicalisation in Holt's thinking was the result of a number of developments. To begin with, by the mid-1970s it was clear to Holt that a transformation of the US educational system to something less coercive was not going to happen. Indeed, as part of a reaction to the 'counter-culture' and 'excess of democracy' of the 1960s the US education system had, if anything, shifted to becoming more authoritarian. This disappointment was married to Holt's growing historical understanding that compulsory schooling has, since its inception, been undergoing an endless process of 'reform' without anything of real significance ever changing. As Holt writes,

> Movements to reform schools never last very long. They soon fall out of fashion, reaction sets in, and most of the new schools that attempt to make humane changes give them up. Usually, when this happens, the public gives a great cry of relief, and all of the long-term failings of the conventional schools *are blamed on the reformers*. (Holt 1976, p. 139)

Holt's clarity about these issues, and his growing understanding of the foundational, irremediable problems with compulsory schooling, stemmed in part from his increasing links to a community of radical scholars and critics of education. Of particular importance in this regard is Holt's friendship with Ivan Illich, the author of *Deschooling Society*, and his time spent at Illich's *Centro Intercultural de Documentación* (CIDOC) in Cuernavaca. As Holt writes in a letter in 1970,

> My short visit to CIDOC has made me feel much more strongly than before that our worldwide system of schooling is far more harmful, and far more deeply and integrally connected with many of the other great evils of our time, than I had supposed. (Holt 1990c, p. 56)

Hence we find that in *Instead of Education*, Holt has shifted away from pedagogy as the site of resistance, to strategies of mutual aid. Through a series of real examples, the book examines how communities can build counter-institutions that 'help people do things better'—that open the world of practices to learners in ways that are compatible with their freedom and autonomy. The examples discussed by Holt in this book include learning exchanges, that offer free courses taught to all-comers by volunteers from the community; community libraries of various kinds of resources (books, of course, but also tools, sporting equipment, etc.); community sporting associations and facilities; community printing presses; community art studios. A particularly important example for Holt in this book is the Peckham Health Centre (which existed in Peckham, London, from 1926 to 1951). Described by Colin Ward as "a unique laboratory of anarchism", this was a highly successful health and social centre in an impoverished area in South London, which was collectively organised and managed by the local community, and made medical knowledge available in a non-paternalistic way (Goodway 2012, pp. 363–5; Pearse and Crocker 1943).

Instead of Education ends with some very practical suggestions for children, to assist them in making their time in school more useful and engaging. One of these suggestions concerns the fun that can be had from school children purchasing their own copy of the teacher's manual. With regard to this, Holt writes that,

4.2 Shifting Strategies

> I can imagine a number of ways in which older children could use the manuals to make school much more interesting. They might, for example, keep a close check on the teacher, to see how closely he stuck to the manual, and in what ways he departed from it. Or they might have some fun at beating the teacher to the draw; thus, if the manual suggested that on a given day the teacher ask a certain question or propose a certain discussion, the children might ask the question or propose the discussion first. Then they could watch the teacher's reactions. Or, where the manual says, 'Have a discussion and bring out this point', they could bring out the point right away, thus ending the fake discussion, or, on the other hand, refuse to bring out the point wanted, no matter how the teacher pushed and prodded. ... I have no qualms at all about suggesting any of this. Any teacher who is dumb and lazy enough to do his teaching out of a manual deserves whatever he gets. (Holt 1976, pp. 216–7)

Of course, this is not just a 'bit of fun', but a practical lesson for school students in resistance and empowerment—in children regaining, through their own activity, power, capacity, and self-respect in the face of the school system's coerciveness. As Holt writes,

> of course, the most important trick in beating the school game is to know that it is a game, as abstract, unreal, and useless as chess, and that beating it *is* a trick. The game is important only because (as with chess) there are rewards for playing it well, and (unlike chess) penalties for playing it badly. (Holt 1976, p. 217)

With his promotion of mutual aid solutions as the most promising form of resistance to compulsory schooling systems, the Holt of *Instead of Education* can thus be seen as part of the anarchist tradition of thought (cf. Ward 2008, Chap. 9). Compare, for example, the 18th century English anarchist William Godwin, who writes in *The Enquirer* that,

> The best motive to learn, is a perception of the value of the thing learned. The worst motive ... may well be affirmed to be constraint and fear. ... If I learn nothing but what I desire to learn, what should hinder me from being my own preceptor?... The boy, like the man, studies because he desires it. He proceeds upon a plan of his own invention, or which, by adopting, he has made his own. (Godwin 1965, Essay IX, pp. 78–80)

And, from the 19th century, consider the following passage from Mikael Bakunin, who writes in *God and the State* that, under anarchism,

> From these schools will be absolutely eliminated the smallest applications or manifestations of the principle of authority. They will be schools no longer; they will be popular academies, in which neither pupils nor masters will be known, where the people will come freely to get, if they need it, free instruction, and in which, rich in their own experience, they will teach in their turn many things ... This, then, will be a mutual instruction, an act of intellectual fraternity. (Bakunin 1970, p. 42, n.)

In *Instead of Education*, Holt shares this anarchist vision of 'schools no longer'—of replacing compulsory schooling with a varied network of resources for 'helping people do things better'. In this way, that 'intellectual fraternity' of which Bakunin speaks is created, not through top-down government policy making and bureaucratic implementation, but through the self-activity of the community. But, unlike Bakunin, who thought this freedom only applicable to adults, for Holt this will be a community of both adults *and* children.

By the time he publishes *Teach Your Own*, Holt's thinking was focussed on the practical strategy of homeschooling (or, to use Holt's term, 'unschooling'). In 1977, Holt had established the newsletter *Growing Without Schooling*, which was intended to be (and became) the information hub of a growing community of homeschoolers. *Teach Your Own* emerged from this activism, and is the first comprehensive discussion of homeschooling in the literature. It contains chapters on the arguments in favour of homeschooling, and replies to common objections. It has extensive accounts (illustrated with lengthy quotations from letters published in *Growing Without Schooling*) of the varied ways in which homeschooling parents and students approach learning—with chapter titles such as 'Learning in the world', 'Serious Play', and 'Learning without teaching'. It also gives detailed advice on dealing with the legal issues involved in withdrawing children from compulsory schooling. In other words, as is typical of Holt's works, *Teach Your Own* is at once a philosophical discussion of the nature of learning, a polemic against compulsory schooling, and a manual for practical action.

It is important to emphasise that homeschooling, as Holt saw it, was not an individualistic rejection of the mutual aid approach outlined in *Instead of Education*, but rather a focussing of that anarchist strategy. The aim was to encourage homeschoolers to build, through their own efforts, a community of mutual support, and the exchange of advice, skills, and resources. Holt thus writes of "this miniature society that homeschoolers are creating—this country within a country, this ancestor (I hope) of a very different, larger society that some of us may someday see" (Farenga and Holcomb, Eds., 1990, p. 33). *Growing Without Schooling* aimed to facilitate this self-activity, but in no way did Holt claim a 'leadership' or 'authority' role within the community. Furthermore, the very act of withdrawing a child from school (which, at this point in US history, was very difficult or even illegal) was itself an example of 'work worth doing'. Through such an act both parents and children would learn and be empowered by becoming aware of their own capacities—to make autonomous choices and see them through, to question authority, to argue for their legal rights, and so forth.

Homeschooling, as envisaged by Holt, was thus an example of precisely the sort of prefigurative politics familiar from anarchist history and theory (see Boggs 1977; Breines 1989). That is, the way in which the movement was organised was itself an attempt to embody (or 'prefigure') the kind of future society it was aiming to create—a community of autonomous, empowered citizens of all ages, who transformed themselves through their own self-activity, without the need for 'authorities' and 'experts' to shape them and their lives. As Holt saw it, the homeschooling movement was, in other words, to be the building of a counter-institution of mutual aid, in opposition to the bureaucratic, authoritarian official education system. We thus find Holt writing in a letter in 1980 that,

> The big picture in the US is discouraging. There are large and visible signs everywhere of a society in a state of collapse. … At the same time there are hundreds of very encouraging small pictures. On a small and local scale Americans are doing a great many interesting, constructive, significant things—building a new and very different society under the shadow of the old. It is with this work and these people that I identify myself. (Holt 1990d, pp. 233–4)

4.2 Shifting Strategies   85

'Building a new and very different society under the shadow of the old': with this (surely deliberate) echo of the famous slogan of the International Workers of the World ('building the new world in the shell of the old'), Holt summarises his hopes for the homeschooling movement that he had done so much to nurture and encourage.

4.3 Homeschooling

How have those hopes been borne out? Writing with the benefit of hindsight, more than thirty years after Holt's death, I would argue that the results are disappointing. If we focus on the situation in the USA, the contemporary homeschooling movement is, in some senses, far more successful than Holt could have dreamed possible. US Department of Education figures suggest that around two million children are now homeschooled (Redford et al. 2017), and the movement has strong political clout (see, e.g., Cooper and Sureau 2007). However, taken as a whole, it has failed to build, as Holt had hoped for, a web of counter-institutions to 'help people do things better'—rooted in collective mutual aid, and accessible to all, rich and poor alike. There are two reasons for this failure.

The first reason is that the homeschooling movement in the USA is overwhelmingly dominated, not by Holt-inspired 'unschoolers', but by evangelical Christians (who make up more than 80% of the total; Kunzman and Gaither 2013, p. 9). Most of the latter have withdrawn their children from school, not because they share Holt's vision of the 'best learning' and a community of autonomous 'do-ers', but because they reject what they see as the liberal and secular worldview of the public school system. The sort of learning that these evangelical homeschoolers provide for their children can be even more narrow and authoritarian, in both form and content, than that found in compulsory schools. The result of such homeschooling can thus be, not an opening of the world to children, as Holt argued for, but an even deeper enclosing of children within the confines of the nuclear family.

This leads me to the second reason for the failure of the homeschooling movement to build counter-institutions. By its nature, homeschooling as a practical strategy focuses on the struggle of each individual family to withdraw its children from compulsory schooling. Although it thereby encourages families to join together as an advocacy group to fight at the political level for such withdrawal to be a legal right, it does not encourage the building of alternative, non-hierarchical institutions through collective action. In other words, homeschooling seeks to extend liberalism's 'sphere of freedom' to children's educational provision, but does not contain within itself the seeds of further mutual aid. Hence, the contemporary homeschooling movement, taken as a whole, is not an engaged, grass-roots resistance to the instrumentalism of contemporary society, but, in some respects, an instance of some of that society's most negative features: the decay of the public realm, and the conception of the neoliberal individual as free from all bonds of social solidarity (cf. Apple 2000; Lubienski 2000). It thus fails to be a fulfilment of Holt's dreams of the beginnings of "a new and very different society". Rather, the contemporary homeschooling movement often seems more like a confirmation of Margaret Thatcher's infamous dictum that "there is no such thing as society, there are individual men and women, and there are families".

If the contemporary homeschooling movement thus fails to embody Holt's broader political hopes, we can still ask whether it is a successful strategy for helping individual children acquire the 'best learning'. The answer to this question has to be *it depends*. To begin with, there is nothing intrinsically about homeschooling that produces such a result. As remarked above, it is perfectly possible for children to be 'homeschooled' in a way that is more authoritarian and restrictive than compulsory education. It should be borne in mind, after all, that school can sometimes be a refuge from parental tyranny. Furthermore, while there is no doubt that there are many homeschooling families who do indeed succeed in providing access to a rich world of practices for their children, this is not something open to all. Unsurprisingly, the homeschooling movement is strongly marked by *class*; it is, overwhelmingly, a middle-class phenomenon (again, see the data in Redford et al. 2017). For if homeschooling is to provide a better environment than the schools for the 'best learning', then this demands that the home in question possess a wide range of resources. This includes money, of course, but also 'cultural capital', confidence in dealing with official bureaucracies, time, energy, and access to the resources required for participation in various practices. By definition, the poor lack money, but they also tend to lack these other important resources. Just consider, for example, the situation faced by many of the poor in the USA at present: impoverished, crime-ridden neighbourhoods; precarious employment at very low wages; food insecurity for more than 10 million children (Coleman-Jensen et al. 2018); a situation in which an unexpected bill (e.g., a medical emergency) can result in homelessness. For people in such circumstances, homeschooling is simply not a viable alternative.

What these considerations entail is that, for many poor children, a reasonably well-resourced public school provides an environment for acquiring the 'best learning' that, despite the limitations discussed in this book, is *far* better than anything that their families, in isolation, could provide for them. For this reason, current attacks in many countries on the public school system by predatory corporate interests (working, e.g., under the guise of 'parental choice') should be opposed even by those who agree with the fundamentals of Holt's critique of our instrumentalised education system. In general, to temper that critique it needs to be borne in mind that school is one of the few public spaces available to children that is not (yet) dominated by commercial motives. It can make available to children easy access to a range of skilled practitioners and resources (in art, sport, inquiry, music, drama, and other practices). Furthermore, for children with physical disabilities, or who are visually or hearing impaired (etc.) access to practices can demand highly specialised resources, which many families could not possibly afford to provide by themselves. Or consider, for example, how in highly patriarchal societies, schools can play a crucial role in opening the world of practices up for girls and women. Of course, as Holt points out, the school is coercive in its overall framework, and within it there are important and systematic limitations to the learner's freedom. But the question is not whether school is a perfect realisation of Holt's ideal (it certainly is not), but whether it is *better* at providing opportunities for the 'best learning' than other alternatives realistically available, here and now, to many children. It is simply an unfortunate fact that, in the absence of a network of non-coercive counter-institutions and resources, for many children the compulsory school—for all its failings and coerciveness—still represents their best option for acquiring the 'best learning'.

4.4 Conclusion

The failure of the contemporary homeschooling movement to achieve what Holt had hoped for is not really surprising. For Holt's vision of learning is, after all, fundamentally opposed to the dominant trends of our time. To make this clear, consider what, in the light of the previous chapters' analysis, he would consider to be the *ideal* or *perfect* learning situation. This would be one in which children would have the maximal opportunity for acquiring the 'best learning', and it would have the following characteristics:

> Children would have easy access to a world of adults engaged in serious, meaningful work—work worth doing, as Holt would put it.
>
> This would, in other words, be a world of varied practices, being undertaken by people with voluntary discipline and a wholehearted love for what they did.
>
> It would be in the context of a broader culture which valued the excellent performance of such practices, along with such qualities as skill and dedication, for their own sake.
>
> By 'easy access' is meant that adults engaged in such serious work can be observed by children, and that there are spaces in those practices for children (and novices in general) to participate in serious work to whatever level is possible for them.
>
> Furthermore, along with access to adults doing serious work, children would also have easy access to a wide variety of resources relevant to such practices (such as art facilities, sporting facilities, tools, workshops, libraries, cultural institutions and the like).

In Holt's own words, this would be a 'doing' society, of which he writes as follows:

> The best and only really good place for do-ers would be a society that does not yet exist. In that society all people, of whatever age, sex, race, etc., could have work to do which was varied and interesting, which challenged and rewarded their skill and intelligence, which they could do well and take pride in doing well, over which they could exercise some control, and whose ends and purposes they could understand and respect. Today, very few people feel this way about their work … In such a society no one would worry about 'education'. People would be busy *doing interesting things that mattered*, and they would grow more informed, competent, and wise in doing them. They would learn about the world from living in it, working in it, and changing it, and from knowing a wide variety of people who were doing the same. But nowhere in the world does such a society exist, nor is there one in the making. (Holt 1976, p. 6)

It seems clear that our present culture, society, and economy are overwhelmingly hostile to this ideal. Holt writes in the passage just quoted that, "nowhere in the world does such a society exist, nor is there one in the making". I would go further, and suggest that some words of George Orwell are apposite to our situation:

"The actual outlook, so far as I can calculate the probabilities, is very dark, and any serious thought should start out from that fact" (Orwell 2000, p. 375). Of course things vary from place to place, but, generalising, the salient features of our modern world include the following. To begin with, a very large amount of the labour—that is, the paid work—done by adults is not meaningful and highly skilled, but rather the reverse: degraded, deskilled, and mind-numbing. What is more, whilst there are still many adults engaged in practices for their own sake (communities of scholars, scientists, artists, craftspeople, and the like), access to such serious work for children (indeed, for novices in general), tends to be very difficult. There are, that is, substantial walls between the world of adults and the world of children. Furthermore, such practices are being undertaken in the context of a broader culture that, increasingly, does not value them for their own sake, but only as instruments for the attainment of external goods—money, status, power. In addition, in many countries the influence of neoliberalism since the 1980s has seen the growing privatisation and enclosure of public resources that could facilitate access to practices (e.g., orchestras, public library systems, art galleries, sporting facilities, etc.). Such neoliberalism combined with galloping credentialism, has in many countries also seriously undermined previous routes of access to certain practices, such as apprenticeships, cadetships, traineeships, and vocational forms of education and training more generally.

In his emphasis on the vital importance, for both adults and children, of work worth doing for its own sake, Holt's view of learning thus runs in direct opposition to the dominant features of our contemporary world. It is in this running against the grain of contemporary society that Holt's views are—despite superficial resemblances—ultimately very different from those of other major philosopher of 'child-centred' learning, John Dewey. Consider the following well-known passage from *Democracy and Education*, where Dewey writes,

> To savages it would seem preposterous to seek out a place where nothing but learning was going on in order that one might learn. But as civilisation advances, the gap between the capacities of the young and the concerns of adults widens. Learning by direct sharing in the pursuits of grown-ups becomes increasingly difficult except in the case of less advanced occupations. Much of what adults do is so remote in space and in meaning that playful imitation is less and less adequate to reproduce its spirit. Ability to share effectively in adult activities thus depends upon a prior training given with this end in view. (Dewey 2004, p. 7)

Holt's ideal for 'best learning'—namely, a world in which children learn 'by direct sharing in the pursuits of grown-ups', rather than in separate 'learning institutions'—is precisely what Dewey rejects in this passage as no longer possible. Dewey's stated reason for rejecting such a world as impossible (for us moderns, if not for 'savages') is that with 'advancing civilisation' there is a widening gap between 'the capacities of the young' and the 'concerns of adults'.

If we look at the typical 'developed' economy today, Dewey's contention looks implausible. Dewey is arguing that, as civilisation 'advanced', more and more sophisticated levels of knowledge and expertise would be required to engage in adult work. However, as just remarked, what we have in fact seen is largely the reverse of this: that more and more adult work has been degraded, so that it demands *less* skill and knowledge of the worker, rather than more (see Braverman 1974 for a classic study of this phenomenon). Indeed, there is good reason to think that, in the decades since Dewey wrote, we have seen a tremendous deskilling of our societies, rather than a growth in 'advanced occupations'. Of course there is a cadre of experts and professionals engaged in work of extraordinary technical sophistication, but if we look at the majority of jobs in many wealthy economies, they involve low-skilled 'service' work (consider typical work in retail, hospitality, and aged care, to name three major areas of employment). A child might struggle to tolerate the mind-numbing tediousness and drudgery of such work, but Dewey's suggestion that such work is 'too advanced' for children's capacities is not remotely persuasive.

In sum, Dewey suggests that schools are required because the *cognitive* nature of adult work (its demands of knowledge and expertise) makes integration of children into that work impossible. Schools, in other words, are an inescapable necessity for any 'advanced civilisation'. Holt—with, I suggest, good reason—rejects any such claim. But it seems clear that for us to build a society in which all—adults and children alike—could join in genuinely meaningful work, would demand a thorough-going remaking of our culture, society, and economy. It would, in other words, demand a new world.

There is thus an important sense in which Holt's critique, unlike Dewey's philosophy of education, is *not constructive*. Holt is not offering some plan to 'reform' or even 'replace' the education system. For Holt, it would be better if we had a 'doing' society and no schools, but that we do not have, and almost all the trends—as he well knew—are going in precisely the opposite direction. Homeschooling may offer palliatives for some of these trends, for some people in some contexts, but, in the final analysis, there is no place that can provide children with a safe shelter from the surrounding world's deep instrumentalism. Ideally, Holt desired a society with no 'space' for education at all—but he is well aware that that would involve a whole-sale reconstruction of the society we have now. (It would entail, for example, a completely different way of organising work, which in turn would entail a completely different way of organising the economy.) And Holt (who was not only a philosopher, but also a deeply experienced campaigner and activist) was under no illusions that any such reconstruction was in the offing—and that, furthermore, proposing utopian plans for it was worth than useless (for, after all, to whom would such plans be addressed?). In this sense, then, for those fundamentally committed to the world as it is, Holt's critique is worse than useless—being, ultimately, neither 'constructive' nor 'reasonable'. For what those words ultimately mean is such people's mouths is: *keeping things much as they are* (cf. Geuss 2014).

But for those of us who can no longer share that commitment—as the world rushes headlong towards ecological, social, cultural, and economic disaster—Holt's vision can help to orientate our thoughts and acts. This is precisely because his account of the 'best learning', and his critique of education, run so directly contrary to the deep instrumentalism that dominates our culture and economy. One way of summing up this point, is to say that Holt's works are a critique of a powerful cultural idea: that education is a *technology*. That is, in Borgmann's definition of that word, that it is "an essentially uninteresting if powerful tool, neutral in its relations to cultural values and subservient to political goals" (Borgmann 1984, p. 35). This can be seen in the way that contemporary debates about learning concern themselves, on the one hand, with the question of the right *means* (such as which pedagogical techniques should be used), and, on the other hand, with the question of the right *ends* (such as what curriculum should be taught). Underpinning this way of structuring the debate is an unquestioned (indeed, unarticulated) assumption that thinking of education as comprising activities that are efficient means to achieve ends is itself unproblematic. That is, it takes for granted that the division into means and ends is a neutral framework which begs no questions, and within which any ('reasonable') position can be taken up.

What Holt's account of the 'best learning' helps us to see is that to take up this instrumentalist framing—with its view of education as a technology—is, implicitly, *already* to have accepted certain substantive views about value and the human good, and to have rendered certain alternative views of that good invisible. The instrumentalist framework entails thinking of human activities as intrinsically, essentially geared towards the efficient production of future goods, which are thus seen as conceptually separable from the activities themselves. As I have argued in previous chapters, this instrumentalism goes along with certain conceptions of agency, pleasure, motivation, and learning. It is thereby of a part with the division of our lives under capitalism into, on the one hand, mere consumption, and, on the other hand, increasingly degraded forms of labour. It encourages a conception of the good life as one spent in activities aimed at external goods—at money, status, power; it is a framework which is corrosive of the excellences, because it systematically offers incentives for developing the vices of the practices; it tends to break our lives and activities into disconnected fragments.

In contrast, Holt's account of learning and education, with its focus on autotelic activity and the virtues of practices, embodies a profoundly different vision of the human good. This vision is a very ancient one, and from its perspective, the instrumentalist model of education and its accompanying assumptions appears as, to use Holt's phrase once more, "the creed of a slave". Holt's vision is concerned with the importance of: self-realisation through work worth doing for its own sake; deep engagement with present activity rather than a focus on future outcomes; replacing resentful dutifulness with the agent's self-transformation through a wholehearted, loving submission to the demands of excellence in a practice. This vision is—as should be obvious, and as was certainly obvious to Holt—in deep opposition to much in our contemporary world.

What is of enduring value in Holt is his combination of this profoundly critical vision, with a deeply pragmatic, common-sense realism. With that realism, what he offers us is not grand utopian plans, but a politics of piecemeal resistance and self-defence—located wherever we are, beginning today. Holt's works can help us to see that the reign of instrumentalism is not total. Even in the most apparently inhospitable places, there are always interstices, gaps, and spaces for the pursuit of autotelic activity by both adults and children, and the nurture of the excellences that such activity brings along with it.

I will end with a story told more than two millennia ago by the great Chinese philosopher Zhuangzi. It can serve as a reminder that the conception of the human

4.4 Conclusion

good that we find in Holt's works has deep roots in human history and culture—which is to say, in *us*, and what we value. And deep roots, after all, are not reached by the frost.[2]

> Qing carved a bell-stand, and when it was completed, all who saw it were astonished as if it were the work of spirits. The Duke of Lu went to see it, and asked by what art he had succeeded in producing it.
>
> "Your subject is but a humble wood carver," was Qing's reply; "what art should I be possessed of? Nevertheless, there is one thing which I will mention. When your servant had undertaken to make the bell-stand, I did not venture to waste any of my power, and felt it necessary to fast in order to compose my mind. After fasting for three days, I did not presume to think of any congratulation, reward, rank, or emolument which I might obtain by the execution of my task; after fasting five days, I did not presume to think of the condemnation or commendation which it would produce, or of the skill or want of skill which it might display. At the end of the seven days, I had forgotten all about myself—my four limbs and my whole person. By this time the thought of your Grace's court for which I was to make the thing had passed away; everything that could divert my mind from exclusive devotion to the exercise of my skill had disappeared. Then I went into the forest, and looked at the natural forms of the trees. When I saw one of a perfect form, then the figure of the bell-stand rose up to my view, and I applied my hand to the work. Had I not met with such a tree, I must have abandoned the object; but my Heaven-given faculty and the Heaven-given qualities of the wood were concentrated on it. Thus it was that my spirit was engaged in the production of the bell-stand." (Zhuangzi 2018, §11; translation modified)

References

Apple, M. (2000). The cultural politics of home schooling. *Peabody Journal of Education, 75*(1–2), 256–71.
Bakunin, M. (1970). *God and the state*. New York: Dover Publications.
Boggs, C. (1977). Revolutionary process, political strategy, and the dilemma of power. *Theory and Society, 4*(3), 359–93.
Borgmann, A. (1984). *Technology and the character of contemporary life: A philosophical inquiry*. Chicago, IL: University of Chicago Press.
Braverman, H. (1974). *Labor and monopoly capital: The degradation of work in the twentieth century*. New York: Monthly Review Press.
Breines, W. (1989). *Community and organization in the New Left, 1962–1968: The great refusal* (revised ed.). New Brunswick and London: Rutgers University Press.
Coleman-Jensen, A., Rabbitt, M. P., Gregory, C. A., & Singh, A. (2018). *Household food security in the United States in 2017*. Economic Research Report No. 256. Washington, DC: US Department of Agriculture.
Cooper, B. S., & Sureau, J. (2007). The politics of homeschooling: New developments, new challenges. *Educational Policy, 21*(1), 110–131.
Dewey, J. (2004). *Democracy and education*. Mineola, NY: Dover.
Farenga, P., & Holcomb, J. P. (Eds.). (1990). *Sharing treasures: Book reviews by John Holt*. Cambridge, MA: Holt Associates.
Ferguson, J. (1990). *The anti-politics machine: Depoliticization and bureaucratic power in Lesotho*. Cambridge: Cambridge University Press.
Geuss, R. (2008). *Philosophy and real politics*. Princeton, NJ: Princeton University Press.

---

[2] To borrow the words of Tolkien (1954, Bk 1, Chap. 10).

Geuss, R. (2014). Must criticism be constructive? *A world without why* (pp. 68–90). Princeton, NJ: Princeton University Press.

Godwin, W. (1965). *The enquirer: Reflections on education, manners, and literature.* New York, NY: Augustus M. Kelley.

Goodway, D. (2012). *Anarchist seeds beneath the snow: Left-libertarian thought and British writers from William Morris to Colin Ward.* London: PM Press.

Gutmann, A. (1999). *Democratic education* (revised ed.). Princeton, NJ: Princeton University Press.

Holt, J. (1970). *What do I do Monday?* New York: E. P. Dutton and Co.

Holt, J. (1976). *Instead of education.* New York: E. P. Dutton and Co.

Holt, J. (1981). *Teach your own: A hopeful path for education.* Liss, Hants: Lighthouse Books.

Holt, J. (1990a). Letter to Ivan Illich, 2/22/73. In S. Sheffer (Ed.), *A life worth living: Selected letters of John Holt* (pp. 147–52). Columbus, OH: Ohio State University Press.

Holt, J. (1990b). Letter to Boston University Students, 2/27/70. In S. Sheffer (Ed.), *A life worth living: Selected letters of John Holt* (pp. 60–5). Columbus, OH: Ohio State University Press.

Holt, J. (1990c). Letter to Students at the Center for Intercultural Documentation, 2/19/70. In S. Sheffer (Ed.), *A life worth living: Selected letters of John Holt* (pp. 56–9). Columbus, OH: Ohio State University Press.

Holt, J. (1990d). Letter to Hartmut von Hentig, 8/25/80. In S. Sheffer (Ed.), *A life worth living: Selected letters of John Holt* (pp. 228–35). Columbus, OH: Ohio State University Press.

Kunzman, R., & Gaither, M. (2013). Homeschooling: A comprehensive survey of the research. *Other Education: The Journal of Educational Alternatives, 2*(1), 4–59.

Lubienski, C. (2000). Whither the common good? A critique of home schooling. *Peabody Journal of Education, 75*(1–2), 207–32.

Orwell, G. (2000). Toward European unity, *Partisan Review*, 1947. In S. Orwell & I. Angus (Eds.), *In front of your nose, 1945–1950. The collected essays, journalism and letters* (pp. 370–5). Boston, MA: Nonpareil Books.

Pearse, I. H., & Crocker, L. H. (1943). *The Peckham experiment: A study of the living structure of society.* London: George Allen and Unwin.

Redford, J., Battle, D., Bielick, S., & Gradey, S. (2017). *Homeschooling in the United States 2012* (revised ed.). Washington, DC: US Department of Education.

Rothermel, P. (Ed.). (2015). *International perspectives on home education: Do we still need schools?* London: Palgrave Macmillan.

Tolkien, J. R. R. (1954). *The lord of the rings.* London: Allen and Unwin.

Ward, C. (2008). *Anarchy in action* (2nd ed.). London: Freedom Press.

Zhuangzi. (2018). The full understanding of life. In *The outer chapters* (J. Legge, Trans.). Available at https://ctext.org/zhuangzi/full-understanding-of-life. Accessed December 2018.